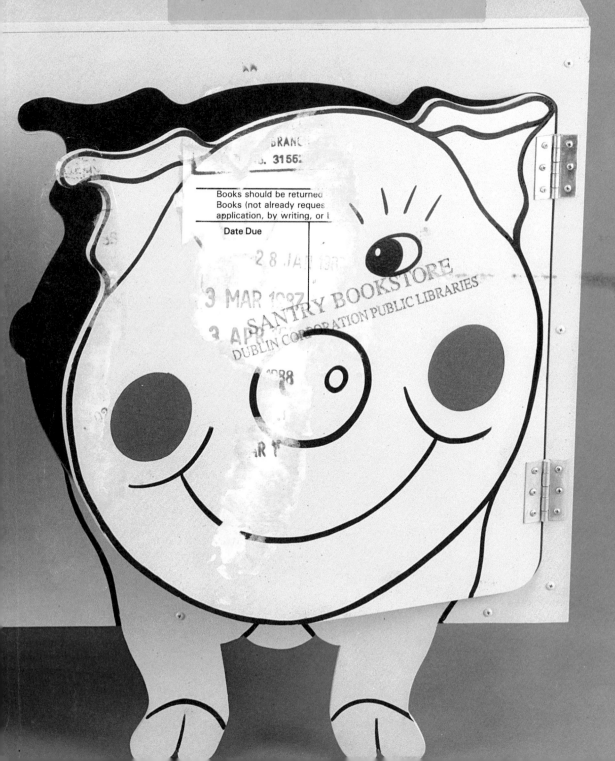

Fun Furniture

WINDWARD

Editor: Fred Milson
Designer: Gordon Robertson
Illustrations: John Hutchinson
Production: Richard Churchill

Published by Windward, an imprint owned by
W.H. Smith & Son Limited Registered No. 237811 England trading as WHS Distributors,
St John's House, East Street, Leicester LE1 6NE

Printed and bound in Italy by L.E.G.O. S.p.A. Phototypeset in the range of Souvenir by Presentia Art, England

ISBN 0 7112 0434 9

© Marshall Cavendish Limited 1986

Contents

Introduction

This part of the book tells you how to go about
building the projects and the tools you will need.

The first part of this book, in these half dozen pages, contains the basic information and describes the working methods that you must use to complete the projects in the second part of the book successfully. So before you browse through to decide on which item you are going to build first, read these pages to acquire an appreciation of how the structures are put together and an insight into what is involved in each particular project. Then you can choose one of the more straightforward ones to start with and go on to something more ambitious like the Old Boot Playhouse or the Dog Eared Table once you have built up confidence in your own technique.

Measurements

All of the dimensions here are quoted in millimetres but in the diagrams, the letters 'mm' have been left off for the sake of clarity.

Most of the projects are based on complete sheets and where the shapes are complicated or difficult, first mark the outline on a grid of squares. The grid itself adds up to 2400mm × 1200mm in most cases, which is slightly smaller than an 8ft × 4ft sheet just in case your sheets are undersized or have damaged corners.

Marking Out

Most of the panels to be marked out have simple straight edges, so the only problem is to get the measurements correct. You will obviously need some sort of giant ruler or 'straightedge' to draw the longer lines with, and you must not rely on a batten for this purpose as they tend

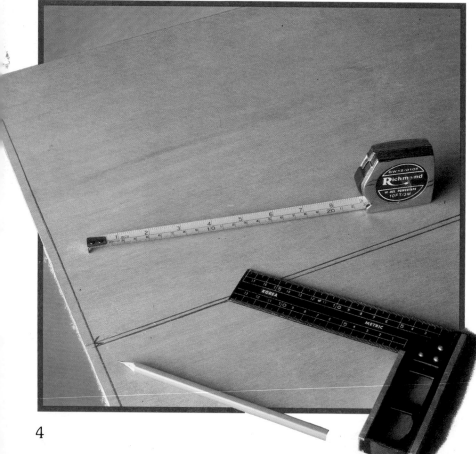

to be very wavy indeed. It is far better to cut a straightedge from one of your sheets as you can rely on the machines to get the edges right.

As for the complicated shapes that make up the sides of most of the units, the only way to get the two sides absolutely identical is to cut out one side and then use that to trace out the other one. When you are doing this, hold the pencil at an angle so that the point runs along the edge of the cut sheet exactly. If you try to hold the pencil upright, the point will trace a line three or four millimetres outside the line that you should be aiming for.

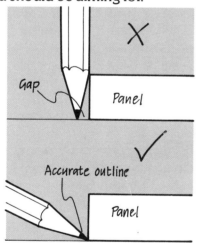

Always mark out on the rough side of the sheet so that when you cut out the panels, the splinters will be on the side that does not show. This means that the panels will end up facing the opposite way round, once you have cut them out.

Sheet Materials

Every one of these fourteen projects is based on the standard 'eight by four' sheet. In metric terms, this is 2440mm × 1220mm. If you are

working in plywood, the 9mm thickness is very strong and this is the material that all the designs here are based on.

The common varieties of plywood are birch-faced and redwood-faced. Birch-faced plywood is very pale in colour, with a light, even grain across the whole surface. This type of grain gives you a surface almost free of splinters and very resistant to water, unlike redwood-faced plywood which is rather open grained and therefore not suitable for use outside in the rain all the year round.

Needless to say, birch-faced plywood is about 25% more expensive than redwood-faced so if you want to make one of these projects for use inside, you can make a worthwhile saving by using the cheaper material. But if you intend to varnish the finished job, use birch-faced because the pale colour is much more suitable for this finish.

When you buy any sheet material, the individual sheets will come off the top of a stack and there is no reason for you to accept the sheets just as they come off the pile. You are entitled to select the sheets that you want to buy and should only accept the really smooth ones with undamaged corners. Many plywood sheets will also have knots showing and during the production process, these knots should all be filled and sanded flat.

Unfortunately the repair material often falls out of the knot holes and leaves an unsightly gash in the panel. The chances are that this blemish will appear on both sides of

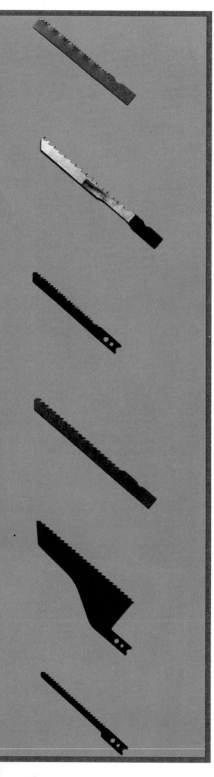

the sheet, so reject any where the knot holes are likely to present a problem at the painting stage.

The obvious alternative to plywood for these jobs is chipboard but this is not as strong as plywood nor will it resist water. So despite the fact that chipboard is roughly 25% of the price of birch-faced plywood, it can only be used for units that are going to be kept in the house. And what is more, you will have to use 13mm chipboard to compensate for the reduced strength so the designs given here will have to be adjusted slightly where there is a partition, where a shelf slides between two battens or wherever a panel fits into a narrow gap.

In some cases, possible problems arising from the use of chipboard have been pointed out on the diagrams but if you miss one of the adjustments, you can probably increase the size of the gap by sawing through the excess piece of the batten carefully with a tenon saw and knocking the surplus wood off with a chisel and mallet.

Chipboard is strong but brittle, so examine the corners of the sheets carefully to make sure that they are not broken before you accept them at the timberyard and if you are taking the sheets away on a roof rack, do not let them hang over too far or the bottom sheet may crack right across due to the weight.

Structure

Though the sheets that make up all these projects are very bendy, the designs are based on simple boxes. So in the same way that a

cardboard box is much stiffer than the cardboard it is made from, these items are very stiff and strong when they are made up because each panel is braced and supported by the neighbouring ones.

In a few cases, notably the slides, the panels are stiffened by extra battens fixed on the underside. If you think that your children are extra rough or extra heavy and you notice that the panels are bending in use, then you can stiffen the units further by adding extra battens.

Tools

Because of the basic simplicity of the designs, you can build all these projects successfully with nothing more than this basic tool kit, plus a jig saw if possible.

8 foot measuring tape
Bradawl or large nail
Screwdrivers
Drill, hand or preferably electric
Drill bits, 9mm – 4mm – 2mm
Sanding block and several grades of sandpaper or Production Paper.
PVA wood adhesive or waterproof glue for exposed conditions
Paint brushes
Sharp pencil for marking out
Try square for right angles

Sawing

All these projects involve a great deal of cutting out and sawing, some of it quite intricate. You cannot get around this, so an electric jig saw is very desirable for working on the smaller projects and almost essential for the bigger ones and the cupboards in particular.

If you are buying a jig saw just for this job, it might be worth paying slightly more to get one with a variable speed facility so that you can adjust it to the material you are cutting. The other feature that would be particularly useful for the front panels is a steerable or scrolling blade so that you can get around the curves more accurately. The final refinement is a pendulum action for the blade, which means that it is only in contact with the wood during the cutting stroke. This gives you a cleaner cut and makes it easier to cut in a straight line. Pendulum action is desirable but not as useful as the other two refinements already mentioned.

The alternative to a jig saw for cutting round the more complicated shapes is to use a coping saw. This has a very thin blade stretched across a light metal frame so that it steers easily around tight corners. The problem with using a coping saw is that you might find it difficult to keep the blade absolutely upright as you work round the corners. You may also find that the metal frame prevents you cutting into the panel beyond a certain point. This does not matter with projects like the Elephant slide, where you can cut away the unwanted wood as you go and so carry on all the way round the shape. But it does matter on the cupboards where you are going to use both the panel and the shape you cut out. With these items, you can only use a jig saw.

If you are only going to use hand tools for the job, you will also need a panel saw to make the straight cuts

with. There is no need to buy an expensive one – the type with a teflon-coated disposable blade would do the job very well indeed.

As for using the jig saw, you must use the right blade for each part of the job. When you are doing the intricate cutting out, use the special thin scrolling blades that steer round corners very easily and do not catch on the sides of the cut.

On the other hand, when you are cutting out the panels, you must use either a metal-cutting blade or one of the fine wood-cutting blades. Do not use a coarse blade as this will tend to catch in the fibres of the material and steer off a straight line. And be careful not to stand on the flex as that will also tend to pull the jig saw off the line.

But even with the correct blade, it is always a problem trying to cut an absolutely straight line with a jig saw. The best way to do it is to use a length of batten fixed to the sheet to guide the sole plate of the jig saw. You can either pin the batten to the sheet with a couple of panel pins or better still, you can hold it in place with a G-clamp at each end. The only difficulty is to allow for the width of the sole plate when you are positioning the batten.

In any case, the golden rule with all power tools is to let them do the work. Do not try to force the blade through the material because that puts pressure on the blade, it bends and so tends to wander off the line.

Always cut on the "waste" side of the line you have marked out on the sheet so that you end up with a panel of the exact size that you

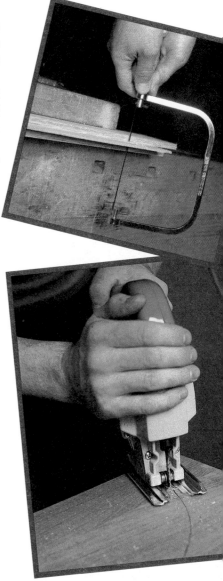

measured in the first place.

When you have finished cutting, smooth off the edges with some coarse sandpaper wrapped around a short length of wood. Then switch to fine sandpaper so that the edges are smooth enough for painting.

Battens

Plywood or chipboard are both too thin to provide a good fixing edge to edge, so all the panels here are joined together by strips of ordinary softwood known as battens, which are screwed and glued to the edges of the panels. The panels are then joined by screwing through one batten into another alongside it.

There is no reason why you cannot also glue as well as screw the panels together to make an even stronger unit. But if you do this, you can never take the units apart again for storage or when you move.

The vast majority of the battens used here are cut from what is known as 2 × 1 PAR. This is on sale in every timberyard but you should buy it with the lengths that you are going to need in mind. For example, if you need four battens roughly four feet long, then it is economic to buy two eight foot lengths of batten but not economic to buy two ten foot lengths because that will leave you with two off-cuts that you will probably never use.

The letters PAR stand for Planed All Round. That means the strips of wood are roughly cut to size and then planed in a separate machine. During the second process, enough wood is removed to leave a smooth finished surface and this varies from

batch to batch. Therefore 2 × 1 PAR is not a fixed size but this has been taken into account in these designs and you do not have to worry about it, provided that all the battens you use come from the same batch of timber. All the batten sizes quoted here are in millimetres.

When you have cut the battens to length, sand the edges and the cut ends lightly. Rounded edges are shown on some battens on the diagrams − this is for safety reasons. Trim the angles with a tenon saw and then complete the rounding off with coarse sandpaper.

Glueing Down the Battens

When you have cut the battens to length, they have to be screwed and glued in place. In most cases, ordinary white PVA woodglue is fine for this sort of work. It is best to buy this in a squeeze pack so that it is easy to apply. With a squeeze pack you can run a line of glue along the batten and then spread it with an old paint brush or a strip of cardboard, whichever is convenient. Wash the brush out with warm water before the glue sets.

The batten can then be screwed into place but if it is twisted at all, you may need to use a couple more screws than allowed for in the instructions if the batten shows any sign of lifting away from the sheet.

It is very important to position the battens correctly but whereas you can trim a bit off the end of a batten if you get the length wrong, it is not possible to adjust the position the other way at all. If you get that wrong, you will have to take the batten right off and re-position it. In that case, you may find that you have to use a new length of batten.

When you are building one of these projects for a really exposed position outside, or when you are putting the roof of the Old Boot Playhouse together, you ought to use a waterproof wood glue.

Painting

In most cases you should not have to worry about any preparation before you start to paint but if you want to achieve a super finish, you can countersink the screwholes. Then paint the screwheads with rustproofing paint, fill them with waterproof filler slightly proud of the panel surface and sand them flat.

Plywood and to a lesser extent chipboard tend to absorb paint but as they normally have a good surface straight from the factory, a coat of oil-based wood primer will seal the surface and start to fill up the blemishes in the grain. Rub down lightly when the primer is dry.

Alternatively, where the finished job is going to be kept out of doors, it might well be worth brushing over the whole thing with a coat of PVA adhesive diluted with water in a one to three ratio. This will seal the surface very effectively and tend to improve the water-resisting properties of the plywood.

Once you have sealed the surface either with PVA or primer, you must paint the whole thing again with undercoat and then the top coat. For outside use, you should put on two top coats or better still use one of the new specially-formulated outdoor paints that resist blistering by stretching with the wood.

Allow the top coat to harden very thoroughly before you mark on and paint the details. Try to use the same brand of paint for both jobs or you might find that you get a reaction between different types of paint. Otherwise you could use the small pots of enamel paint sold for model makers as they tend to be compatible with most types of paint. If you have to use different types of paint, try a test on a concealed patch of the top coat before you go ahead with all the details. Wrinkles or an 'orange peel' effect indicate that there is a reaction.

If you do not want to go to the trouble of an elaborate paint job, you could use a combined varnish and stain instead. Do not use a polyurethane-based varnish.

Where the finished unit will be kept outside, it is best to seal the gaps between the panels with mastic, but make sure that the type you use will take paint.

Warning
All the designs in this book are at least as strong as the furniture you can buy in the shops, provided that you follow the instructions exactly. But if you have any doubts, we advise you to ask an experienced woodworker to check over the finished product before you put it into use.

We also advise you to make sure that the paint you use is lead-free and approved for use in places where children may chew the finished surface.

Camper Bunk Beds

The streamlined Camper provides sitting and storage during the day and a pair of bunks at night.

Materials

2 sheets 2440mm × 1220mm 13mm chipboard PLUS 3 sheets 2440mm × 1220mm 9mm plywood OR 5 sheets 2440mm × 1220mm chipboard.

Battens

Cut from 25mm × 50mm PAR

2 ×	1044mm	A
2 ×	1066mm	B
2 ×	484mm	C
2 ×	686mm	D
2 ×	330mm	E
2 ×	1714mm	F
2 ×	2286mm	G
3 ×	229mm	H,J
1 ×	635mm	K
3 ×	710mm	L,P,R
3 ×	660mm	M,N,Q
1 ×	292mm	S

22m of battening, allowing for waste.

100 25mm no.8 pan-head screws.

2 75mm hinges.

12 25mm no.10 countersunk woodscrews.

The Camper bunk bed is much more exciting than the normal accommodation for a couple of kids, and the unit only takes up a little more room than the everyday design. So although the whole thing is around 18 inches longer than usual, it does have a large tray on the top deck to take a bedside light and a supply of books and soft toys while the bottom deck allows the driver to sit down and work things out carefully at a writing desk.

If you want to screw the Camper to a wall, take ten minutes to work out the best way round for the driver to face so that plenty of light falls on the desk top. Once you have decided that, you can work out which side to fit the door in so that it faces out into the room. There is no problem about this, you just have to draw the plans on the chipboard or plywood in reverse if necessary.

Marking Out

If you want the bed to face left to right as it does in the photograph, you will need to cut out the first side complete with the door exactly as it appears on the plan in Fig.1. If you

want it to face the other way, you will have to cut out the side with the door the other way round

Mark out the outside shape and the shape of the apertures to be cut out on the inside (rougher) face of one of the side panels. The windows you cut out will be waste material as far as the bed is concerned, but they may come in useful for another job later. Then drill a 9mm diameter hole close to the inside of the line in each aperture so you can start sawing except in the door, where you can drill the hole in the cut out for the finger hole.

All the rounded corners of the panels and the apertures can be marked out around the base of a standard aerosol paint can, or something else which has a diameter of about 65mm. When one of the side panels has been cut out, use it as the basic pattern for marking out the other side panel.

Mark out a line the full length of the side panels 50mm down from the top edge as shown in Fig.2. This will help you to locate the top of battens A and D and the top edge of batten C later. You can now go

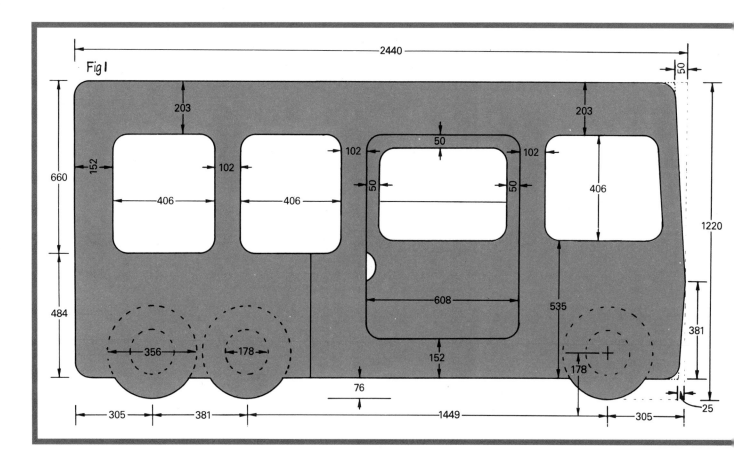

Fig I

ahead to mark and cut out the rear panel, see Fig.3, the windscreen panel, the radiator panel and the partition, see Fig.4. Remember to drill your starter holes in the apertures, close to the inside of the line.

The headlamps do not need to be precisely 127mm in diameter, so mark them out round a saucer or paint tin of approximately that size. However, do make sure that the gap between the side of the panel and the outside edge of the headlamps is at least 38mm so that there is no chance of the material breaking and that the bottom of the lower headlight rim is at least 50mm up from the bottom of the panel.

Battens

Cut the various battens to the lengths shown at the beginning of this section. Round off one end of battens A and B. All the battens will be fixed to the INSIDE faces of the panels, the same face on which you have done your marking out.

Now drill a series of 4mm diameter fixing holes through the 50mm face of each batten. The actual location of these holes is not all that important except in the case of batten K where they should not be drilled less than 25mm in from either end – otherwise they will get in the way of the screws for the door hinges. In other cases, you will need

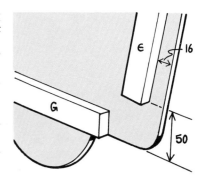

a hole 50mm in from each end and the others spaced at 300mm to 450mm intervals.

Fix the battens to the side panel with the door in it first. Apply adhesive to the 50mm face of the batten that will be in contact with the panel and work on one batten at a time.

Locate the rounded top of batten A 50mm down from the top of the panel (touching the line you marked out) and 16mm in from the rear edge. Screw down.

Locate the rounded top of batten B, flush with the top of the panel and 70mm up from the bottom edge in such a way that its rear edge is flush with the edge of the door aperture, 1766mm in from the rear edge of the panel. Screw down the batten.

Locate batten C with its top edge 50mm down from the top of the panel and leaving a 13mm gap between its rear end and the front edge of batten B. Screw down.

Locate batten D so that its front edge is 16mm in from the front of the panel and so that its uppermost corner is 50mm down from the top of the panel, level with the top edge of batten C. Screw down.

Locate batten E so that its front edge is 16mm in from the front of edge of the panel and with its bottom-most corner 50mm from the bottom of the panel. Screw down. Locate batten F approximately centrally between battens A and B and with its lower edge flush with the top of the window and door apertures (203mm down from the top edge of the panel). Screw down. Locate batten G centrally between battens A and E so that the gap at each end is even and with its lower edge flush with the bottom edge of the panel, 76mm up from the bottom of the wheels.

The height of the batten for the desk and seat shown in Fig.2 may be changed according to the size of the children who will use them. However, battens (H) should be at least 25mm below the bottom edge of the front window and there must be a gap of 13mm between the back end of batten J and the front edge of batten B to allow the partition to slide down between the two battens. Make sure you fix batten H in the same position on both side panels. Batten J is only fixed to one side panel. If you want right hand drive and the bus faces right to left, batten J goes on the side with the door in it. If you want left hand drive, it goes on the side without the door. If the bus faces left to right the position is reversed. Locate batten K, on the inside of the door, flush with the front edge of the door and with its top 75mm down from the top of the door. Screw down.

Repeat these procedures for the other side panel except that batten

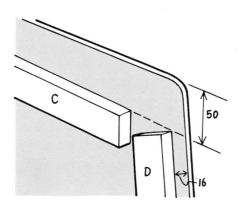

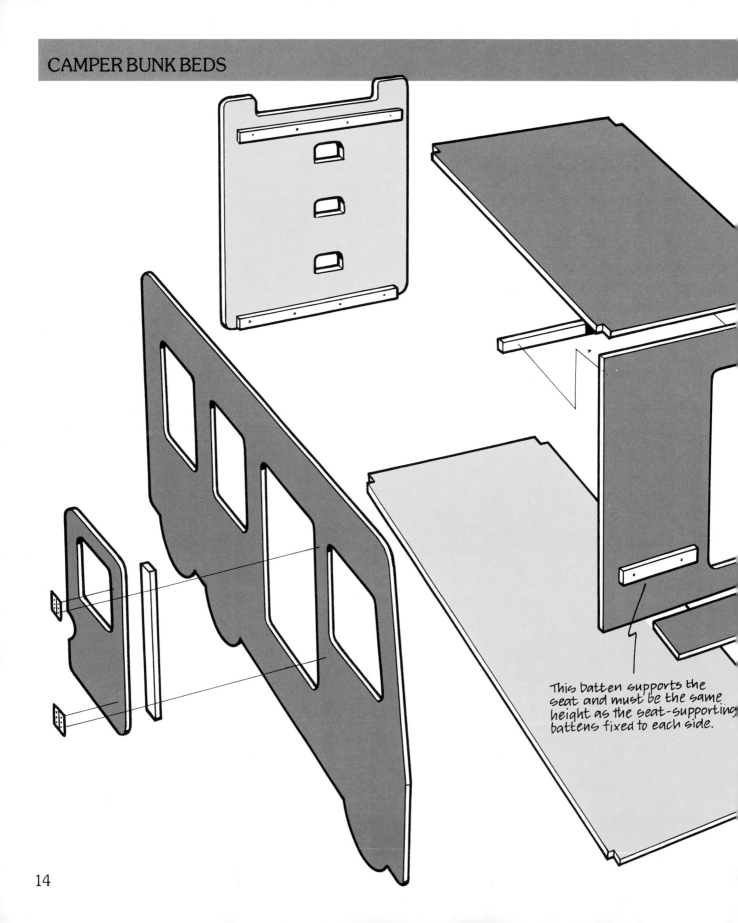

This batten supports the seat and must be the same height as the seat-supporting battens fixed to each side.

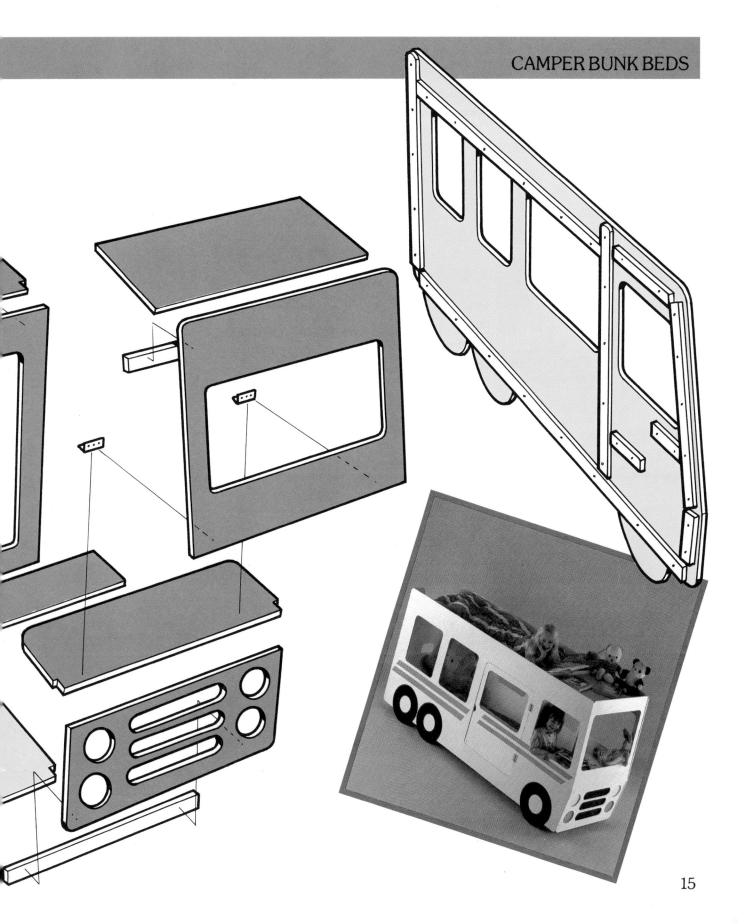

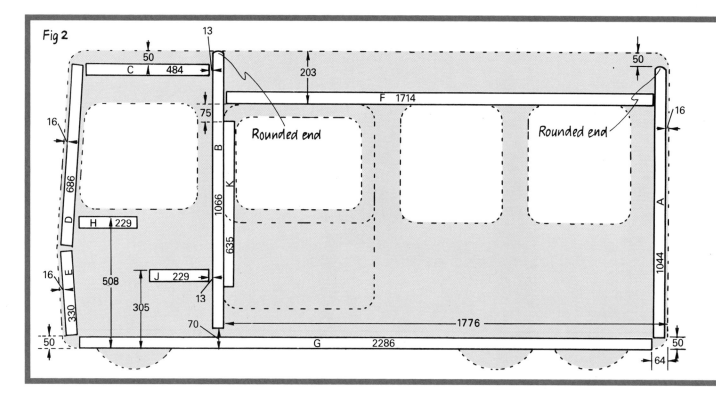

Fig 2

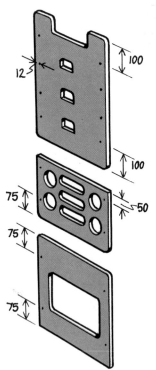

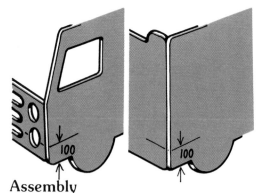

B will have its back edge flush with the front of the second window aperture, 1892mm in from the rear edge of the panel. On the end panels, battens L, M, N, and Q should all be located centrally, leaving 25mm at either end in the case of batten L and 50mm at either end in the case of battens M, N and Q. Battens M, N and Q will be flush with the bottom of their respective panels while the bottom of batten L will be 203mm down from the top of the panel.

When the adhesive is dry, you can begin assembly. Drill a series of 4mm diameter holes 12mm in from the edges of the three end panels.

As a guide during assembly, mark a line on the ends of both side panels 100mm up from the bottom and 100mm down from the top. Mark a line on the outside of the radiator panel and on the outside of the rear panel 100mm up from the bottom as well.

Assembly

You will need some assistance during this stage. Get a helper to hold one of the side panels upright while you position the rear panel in place,

Mark line on windscreen panel level with top of batten C

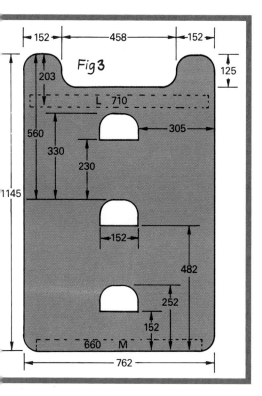

Fig 3

D and between the side panels. Now mark a point on each side of the inside of the windscreen panel level with top of battens C.

These marks will show you the position of the *top* of batten P which can now be glued and screwed in place. The top of batten P will be approximately 717mm up from the bottom of the windscreen panel but this will depend on the size of the battens. You do not need to wait for the adhesive to dry. Go ahead and screw the windscreen panel to battens D, so that its bottom edge is resting on the top edge of the radiator panel.

If you want the Camper to be right hand drive, Fig.4 shows you the front view of the partition. Batten S should be fixed with its top edge at the same distance from the top of the panel as batten J is from the top of the side panel and 25mm in from the *edge* of the panel. It is fixed to the *front* of the partition. Batten R is then located centrally with its bottom edge 203mm down from the top of the panel on the *back* of the partition. Screw and glue both the battens into place.

If you want the Camper to be left hand drive, put the aperture on the left and batten S on the right as you look at it.

You can now drill three 4mm diameter holes, 12mm in from each edge and evenly spaced. Slide the partition down between battens B and J. Screw it into batten B from the front in such a way that the top of the partition is level with the top of the side panels otherwise your seat batten won't line up.

lining up the two marks you made at the bottom of the panels.

Screw the rear panel to batten A. Now, get your helper to hold the other side panel up in such a way that your marks line up and screw the other side of the rear panel into batten A in the other side panel. Once this is done, the unit should stand up by itself and the top and bottom edges of the rear panel should be level with the top and bottom edges of the side panels.

You can now screw the radiator panel in place, lining up your marks so that the bottom of the radiator panel is level with the bottom of the side panels. Screw into place at both sides. Next, position the windscreen so that it is sitting on top of the radiator panel against battens

You can now measure up for the desk top, the decks and the shelf. The desk top is just an oblong with cut-outs to allow for the battens. To find the lengths of the chipboard panels for the decks and shelf, measure (1) the distance between the inside face of the radiator panel and the inside face of the rear panel (2) the distance between the rear face of the partition and the inside face of the rear panel and (3) the distance between the inside of the windscreen panel and the front face of the partition. This will give you the lengths of the lower deck, the upper deck and the shelf.

When you have cut your chipboard to size, cut out the corners to allow for the battens and drill a series of 4mm diameter holes along each edge, 12mm in from the edges and at approximately 450mm intervals. Take off the partition, the windscreen panel and the radiator panel. Pull the front of the side panels apart slightly and slide the lower deck in from the front along the top of batten G until it sits on top of batten M at the back.

Pull the front end of the side panels together again. The front edge of the chipboard should now be flush with the front edge of batten E if you have measured it right! If it is, then re-fix the radiator panel so that the base sits on top of batten N. You can now screw through the base into battens G, N and E making sure that the side panels are pulled well together in the middle so that there is no gap between the edge of the chipboard and the inside face of the side panels. Screw

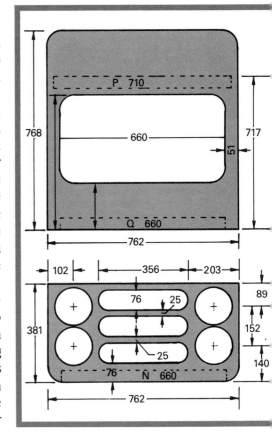

the windscreen panel and partition back into their original position.

Now cut out the seat panel measuring 230mm × 300mm and a radius round one corner with an aerosol can. Measure the distance from the top of batten (J) or (S) to the top of the chipboard base. Then cut a length of batten to this size. This will be the leg of the seat. You will then need two other battens, one 180mm long and the other one 225mm long.

Locate the battens on the underside of the seat, mark round them and then drill two holes for each through the seat, making sure that the screw holes are in the middle of

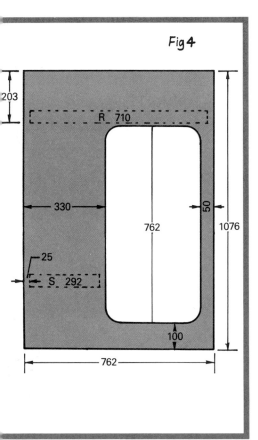

Fig 4

203
R 710
330
762
50
1076
25
S 292
100
762

headlamps and grill on the hardboard and paint them in before fixing the grill in place.

To fix the hinges to the door and door frames, first mark a line 150mm down from the top of door aperture on the door frame, then another line 275mm up from the bottom of the panel. These will indicate the position of the top of the top hinge and the bottom of the bottom hinge.

Place a couple of jig saw blades on the bottom of the door aperture and sit the door on top of them. This will give you the necessary gap at the bottom of the door to allow for opening. Mark out the position of the screw holes. Make starter holes and drill as before, then screw on the hinges.

The carpentry for the Camper bed is now complete. All that remains is to paint it and make up suitable mattresses.

Use high-density upholstery foam for the interior of the mattress. Take the measurements along with you to the shop as they will usually supply the foam cut to size. Make the covering for the mattress from a polyester material so that you can wash it out easily.

If you are going to stand the bed against a wall, it is a good idea to stabilise it by bolting it to the wall through batten F, using a couple of rawlbolts or something similar. If there is a skirting board at the foot of the wall, you will need to put a spacer block between the bed and the wall at the fixing points, the same thickness as the skirting board to keep it upright.

where the battens will go. Screw and glue these battens in place, screwing through from the top of the seat. The dotted line shows where the leg will go. Drill two 4mm diameter holes for fixing screws and then screw and glue the leg in place.

Now drill a couple of holes 12mm in from the edge that will fit over battens J and S so that the seat can be fixed firmly in place.

For the backing to the radiator panel, you will need a piece of hardboard (or use some plywood or chipboard off-cuts) 330mm × 712mm. Lay this, shiny face up, on two bits of batten off-cut, then lay the end panel on top. Mark out the

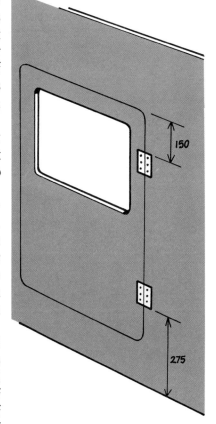

150

275

Bus Bed with Desk

A double decker with a difference. Sleep on the top deck, work and store your luggage on the bottom one.

The Bus is a double decker that provides a proper bed on the top deck and a storage cupboard plus a writing desk on the bottom one. The side of the bus has a hatch cut in it to allow the driver access to the desk, and a doorway for the cupboard. You can position these either side of the vehicle, while the steps to the upper deck can be cut in the same side or in the back panel.

Depending on the amount of room available, you can either build the bus completely free-standing or you can fix it to a wall through one of the top battens. If you decide to fix the Bus to the wall, work out the best way round to position it so that plenty of natural light falls on the desk from the window.

Take the instructions for fixing the Bus Bed to the wall and for making suitable mattresses from the end of the chapter on the Camper.

Marking Out

When you have decided on the direction that the Bus is going to face, you can work out how you are going to cut out the panels so that the Bus faces in the right direction.

As the basic outline of each side is identical, you just have to cut out sides the other way round if you want the Bus to face in the opposite direction to the one shown in the pictures.

By marking out the sides according to their eventual position, the hatch, the cupboard door and the steps should end up in the side away from the wall. Then you can either cut out the hatch on the other side to half the height to prevent things falling down between the side of the bus and the wall, or cut it out to the same size to give a door at each side if you intend the bus to be free standing. The dotted line on the plan indicates the half-size hatch.

Transfer the outline of the sides from Figs.1 and 2 on to the sheet with a ball-point pen and then mark in all the apertures carefully. There is no need to worry about getting the rounded corners marked correctly to start with, just position the straight lines accurately and then mark out the rounded corners by joining up the straight lines with a curve. The best way of getting a regular curve in all the corners is to

Materials

3 sheets 2440mm × 1220mm 9mm exterior grade plywood PLUS 2 sheets 2440mm × 1220mm chipboard OR 5 sheets 2440mm × 1220mm chipboard.

Battens

Cut from 25mm × 50mm PAR

2 ×	1044mm	A
2 ×	406mm	B
2 ×	180mm	C
2 ×	1702mm	D
2 ×	864mm	E,F
2 ×	724mm	G
2 ×	965mm	H
2 ×	512mm	J
3 ×	457mm	K,Q
2 ×	432mm	L
6 ×	152mm	M,N,P
3 ×	710mm	R,T,W
2 ×	660mm	S,V

20m battening, allowing for waste.
100 Panhead screws.
2 75mm hinges.

use the base of something like an aerosol can for the larger corners, and a coin for the smaller ones. Do not try to cut the corners square as it is very difficult to get a good finish on a square corner and they also tend to be less strong.

Once you have got the technique worked out, go on to cut out the outline of the rear panel, the front top panel, the windscreen panel, and the radiator panel as in Fig.3. The diameter of the headlamps does not have to be exactly 102mm, providing there is a gap of at least 25mm between the rim of the headlamp and the edge of the panel.

Finally, cut out the shapes for the partition, desk, seat and shelves. It might be worth strengthening these with battens if you are working in chipboard but in all cases, you must use strengthening battens underneath the panel for the seat.

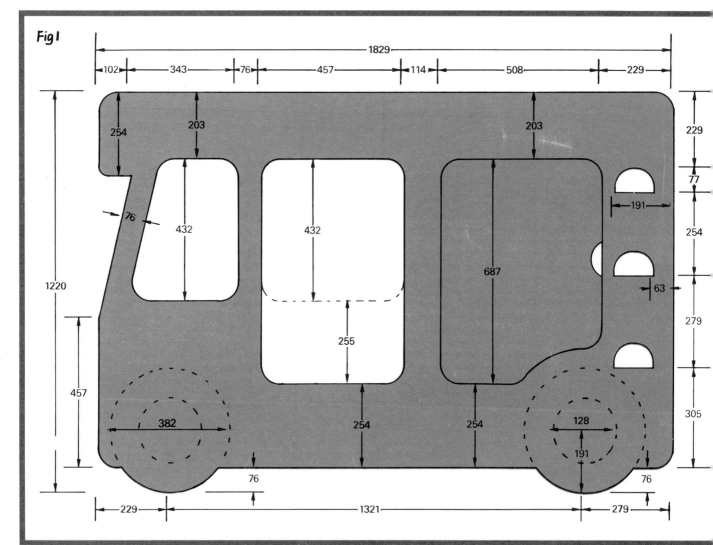

Fig 1

Battens

Cut the battens out of 25m x 50mm PAR to the lengths given at the beginning of this section. Sand and bevel all the edges and corners as required. All the battens except batten W have to be drilled with 4mm diameter fixing holes through their 50mm face. They should all have holes 50mm or so in from either end and then at 300mm to 400mm intervals all the way along.

Using a cheap 25mm paintbrush or an off-cut of hardboard, apply adhesive to the 50mm face of the battens that will be in contact with the panels. Start with batten A on the side panel, positioning it 13mm in from the rear edge of the panel, with the top and bottom ends 50mm from the top and bottom of the panel.

Next, fix batten B 13mm in from the front of the panel and with its

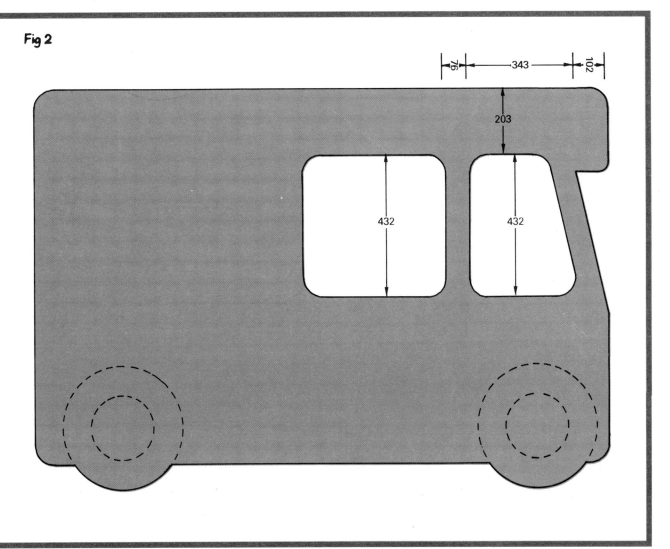

Fig 2

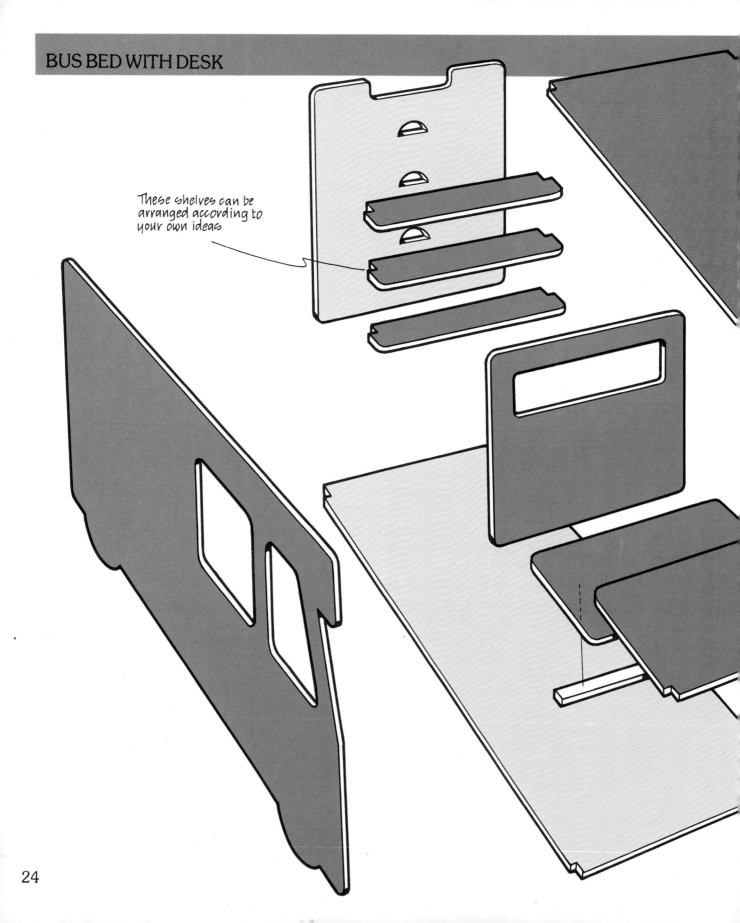

These shelves can be arranged according to your own ideas

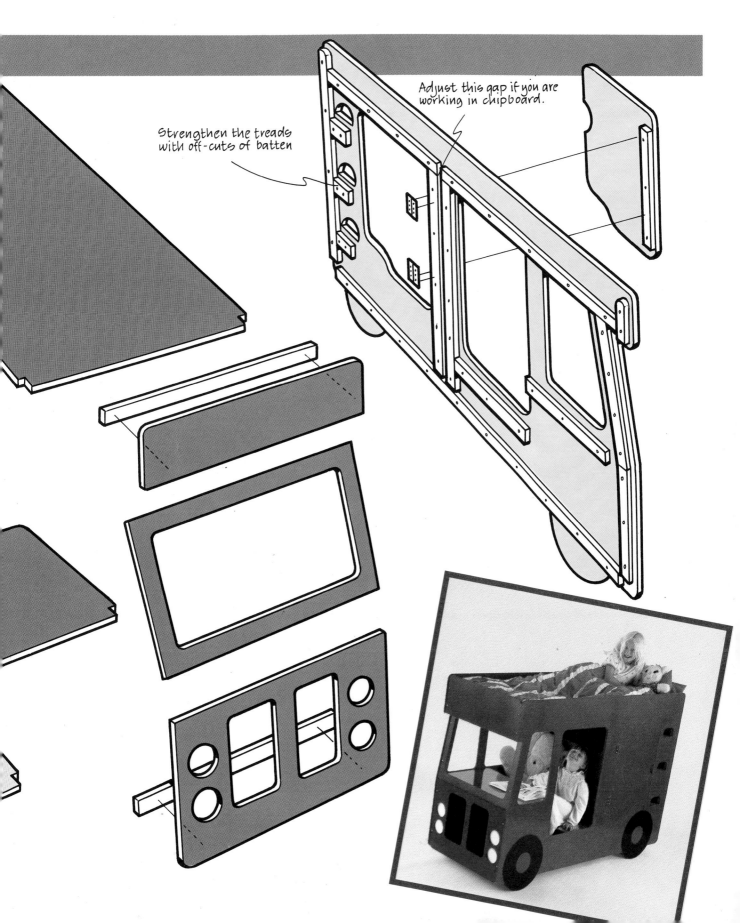

Strengthen the treads with off-cuts of batten

Adjust this gap if you are working in chipboard.

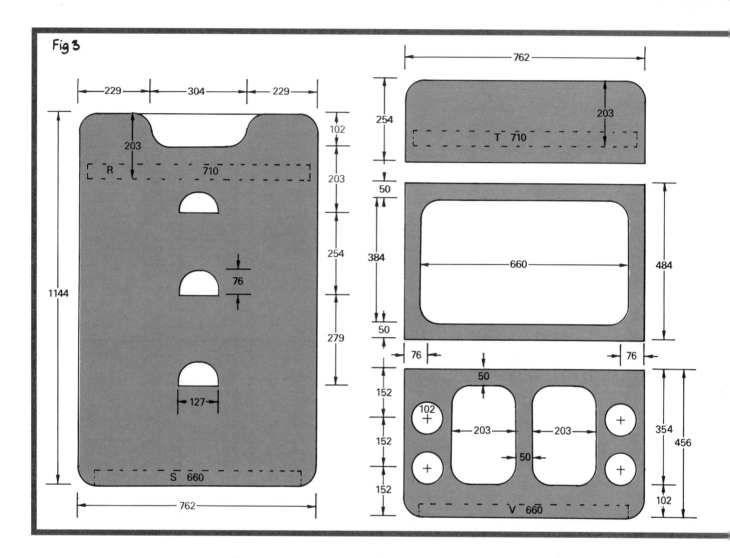

Fig 3

bottom end 50mm up from the bottom of the panel. Fix batten C 13mm in from the front of the panel and with its top end 50mm down from the top of the panel – level with the top of batten A. Fix batten D in position approximately midway between battens A and B and with its lower edge flush with the bottom of the panel.

In Fig.4, battens E and F are separated by a 12mm gap into which the partition will eventually slide. Since the material you are using for the partition is only 9mm thick, this will at first produce a rather loose fit. However, once both battens and partition have been painted, the problem will tend to disappear. If it remains loose, you can line the gap with thin felt at the final stage. If you are working in chipboard, remember to open this gap up to 15mm at each side to allow for the extra thickness of the material.

Position batten F so that its rear

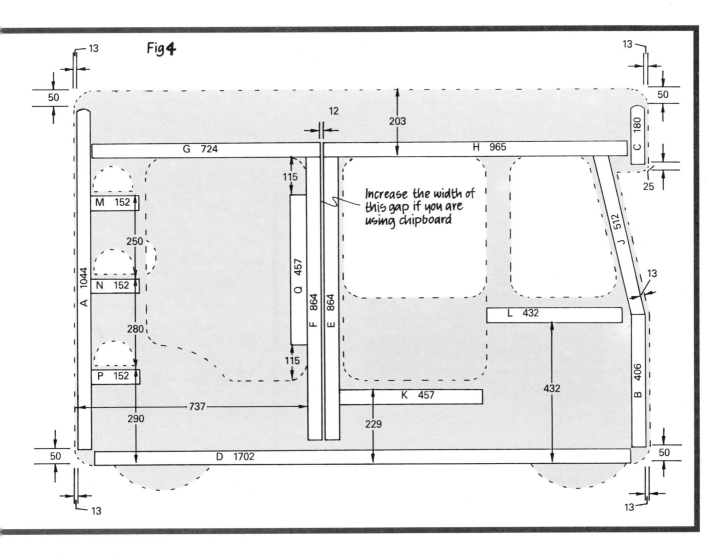

Fig 4

Increase the width of this gap if you are using chipboard

edge is flush with the front of the cupboard door opening. On the side with no cupboard door draw a vertical line 737mm in from the rear edge of the panel, and fix batten F so that its rear edge is on this line. Glue and screw batten F in position in such a way that its top is flush with the top of the cupboard aperture or 203mm from the top of the bus. This should mean that there is a gap between the bottom of batten F and the top of rail D of about 25mm into

which the chipboard floor will eventually slide.

Batten E can now be fixed in place. Top and bottom should be level with the top and bottom of batten F. Since the distance from the back edge of batten F to the back of the middle hatch is 114mm and since the battens will have been planed to less than their original 50mm, the front edge of batten E will NOT be flush with the rear edge of the middle hatch. This does not matter so long as the gap between battens E and F is correct.

The upper rail, batten G, can now be screwed and glued in place in such a way that its UNDERSIDE is flush with top of the cupboard door, or 203mm down from the top of the bus. In this position it should sit on top of batten F and its front edge should be flush with the front edge of batten F. In other words, it should not be allowed to intrude into the gap which you have already formed to support the partition.

Next, position batten H with its underside flush with the top of the middle hatch and its rear end 12mm or 15mm from the front end of batten G. This will leave a small gap between the front end of rail H and the back edge of batten C. This does not matter at all.

Batten J fits between batten B and batten H. Lay it into place and mark the ends with a pencil so that you can saw the ends to fit neatly. Otherwise the only important thing about batten J is to make sure that it is positioned 13mm in from the front edge of the panel.

To complete the sides, it only remains to fix the shelf battens and the battens to support the desk and seat, as shown in Fig.4. Although suggested positions for desk and seats are shown on the plans, their actual location is a matter of choice, their height depending on the size of the child who will use the bus. Remember, however, to leave a gap of at least 13mm between the top of the seat and desk battens K and L and the bottom of the apertures. When you are deciding where to position the shelves in the cupboard, ensure that they do not interfere with the footholds in the side or the rear panel.

Fix battens R and S to the inside of the rear panel, as shown on Fig.3. Batten S should be flush with the bottom of the panel and 50mm or so in from either side. The bottom

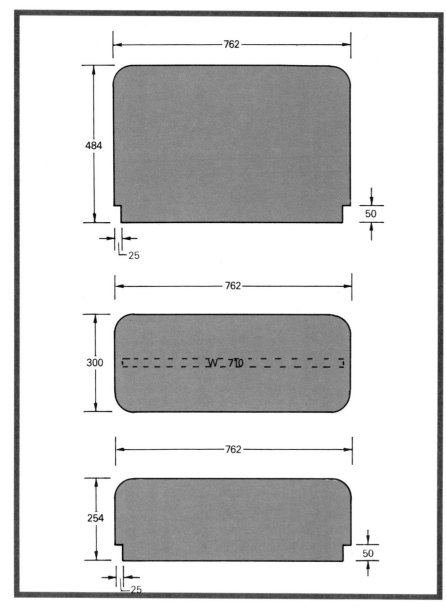

edge of batten R should be 203mm down from the top of the panel and with a gap of about 25mm at either end, clear of the top step.

Fix batten T to the inside face of the front top panel so that its bottom edge is 203mm down from the top of the panel. It should have a gap of about 25mm at either end, see

Fig.3. Fix batten V to the inside face of the radiator panel, so that its bottom edge is flush with the bottom of the panel. There should be a gap of about 50mm at either end.

Now go back to the seat panel. Drill a row of three 4mm diameter holes in the seat and then apply adhesive to one of the 25mm faces

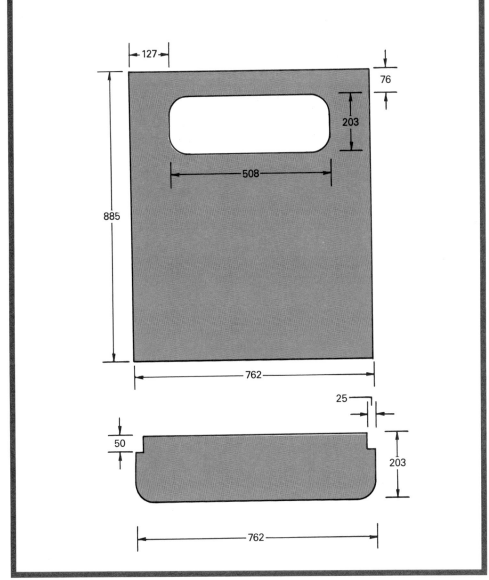

of batten W. Position W in the middle of the panel and screw through the seat into it from the top.

The top and bottom bases are cut from chipboard in all versions. Measure the exact sizes required and make cut-outs in the corners to allow for the battens. When the chipboard has been cut out drill a row of 4mm diameter holes at 300mm intervals or so along each side 12mm in from the edges. The panels must now be sanded off, especially round the edges and apertures and also painted before you go any further.

You will then need a piece of hardboard 350mm × 700mm, which should be painted black and stuck to the inside of the radiator panel to close it off and prevent the children poking things through.

Drill a series of 4mm diameter holes, 12mm in from the vertical edges of the front and rear panels so that you can screw the bus together.

Assembly

For the assembly, you are going to need somebody around to help you. Mark a point on the front and rear edges of the side panels 100mm up from the bottom of the panel. Then, draw a line on the outside faces of the rear and radiator panels, 100mm up from the bottom of the panels.

Get your helper to hold one of the side panels upright while you position the rear panel so that your marks line up. Screw through the rear panel into batten A. Repeat this procedure for the other side panel and the unit will now stand up by itself. Slide the floor into position from the front in such a way that it sits on top of batten D. Your helper will have to pull the sides apart slightly at the front while you do this. Once the base is in position push them together.

You can now line up your marks on the radiator panel and screw

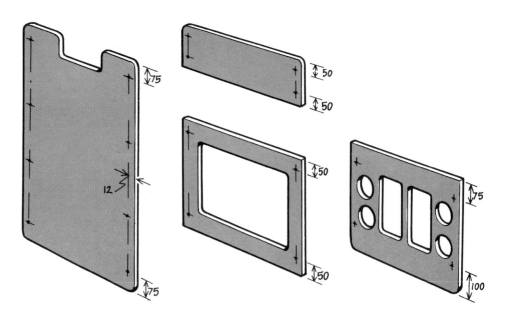

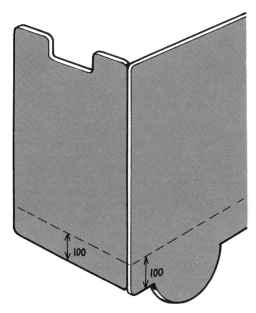

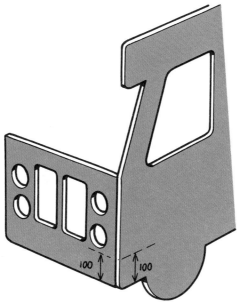

through into battens B. Next, fix the windscreen so that it sits on top of the radiator panel. Finally, fix the top panel, making sure that its top edge is level with the top edge of the side panels.

Pull the sides together so that there is no gap between the edges of the floor and the inside faces of the side panels. Squeeze some wood adhesive along the edges of the floor if you want to make the unit really strong. Screw the floor into the battens all round.

Now slide the partition down between battens E and F and position the shelves, desk and seat. These do not need to be screwed down, although with the exception of the seat, they can be if desired. The battens on which the seat rests are longer than the seat itself. This is so that the seat can slide backwards and forwards a little as necessary.

Sit the bed-base on the top of

battens G and H and screw down all round, making sure the sides are pulled together first.

The door should have batten Q fixed at its front edge. This batten will carry the hinges. First screw the

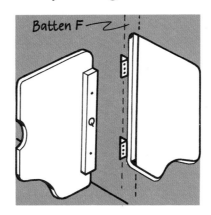

hinges to the side panels then offer up the doors and mark the position of the screw-holes. Make guide holes with a nail and then screw the hinges onto the door. Make sure screws do not go right through.

Jeep Desk

Four wheel drive cars are becoming more popular. Here is a four wheel drive Desk with storage space as well.

Materials
2 sheets 2440mm × 1220mm
9mm exterior quality
plywood OR 2
sheets 2440mm × 1220mm
chipboard.

Battens
Cut from 25mm × 50mm PAR
2 × 394mm   A
2 × 381mm   B
2 × 406mm   C
2 × 356mm   D
2 × 1092mm E
4 × 508mm   F,L,M
3 × 710mm   G,H,N
2 × 660mm   J,K
12m battening, allowing for a
little waste.
2 75mm hinges.
50 25mm panhead screws
(galvanised or plated).

The Jeep desk is an ideal place to sit and read, either on your own or with a friend depending on whether you decide to build the wide or narrow version. In both cases there is a shelf at the back for other books to keep the main working surface clear, while the boot offers plenty of storage space as well.

Like the real thing the Jeep desk is small and compact, so this is an ideal project to choose if you only have a limited amount of room for toys inside the house. On the other hand, if you take the precaution of building the Jeep out of exterior-grade plywood, the desk is small enough to be lifted in and out of the house so that it can be used in the garden and left outside for the whole summer without losing its good looks too obviously.

Marking Out
The best way to work is to mark out the floor, the seat-back, the boot panel and the seat on one sheet and cut both sides, the rear shelf, the bonnet and the radiator panel from the other, as shown below.

The width of 761mm shown in the drawings enables two children up to about the age of 6 years old to sit side by side. If the desk is only to be used by one child, then it need only be 611mm wide. In this case you will have to reduce the overall width shown in Figs. 2 and 4 and the length of battens G, H, J, K, and N by 150mm. You will also need to make some adjustments to the radiator grill. Instead of having 4 slots 70mm wide, separated by a gap of 25mm, you could have 2 slots 70mm wide separated by a

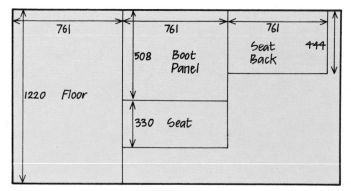

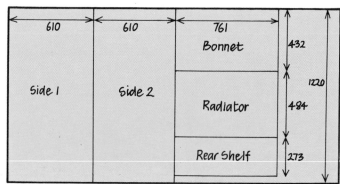

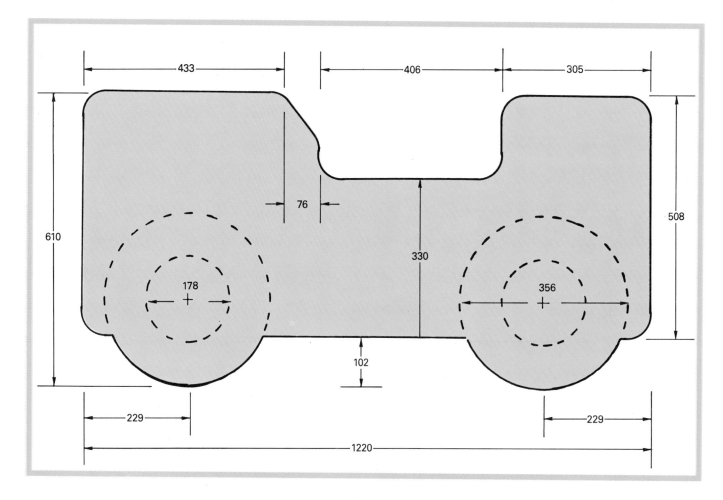

gap of 65mm. The headlamps must stay in the same place relative to the top and outside edges.

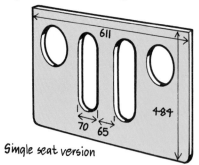

Single seat version

Mark out one side panel first using the plan in Fig.1. Then, when you have cut it out, use it as a pattern for the other side panel, which is identical. All the panels should be rounded off in the usual way. Now mark out all the other panels except the floor which comes later. The headlamps do not need to be exactly 127mm in diameter, so long as there is at least 50mm between their rim and the side of the panel and so long as the top of the rim is level with top of the grill openings.

Drill a 9mm diameter hole close to one of the inside edges of each headlamp and radiator grill opening and another in the finger hole of the boot so you can cut them out later.

Battens

Cut your battens to the lengths shown at the beginning of this section, sanding all the edges and corners to a slight bevel to eliminate splinters.

Drill a series of 4mm diameter holes through the 50mm face of each batten. One hole should be 50mm in from either end except in the case of battens L and M where the holes should be 25mm in from either end and one approximately in the middle. The other exception is batten E where apart from the end holes there should be 2 or 3 evenly spaced fixing holes.

Taking one panel and one batten at a time, apply adhesive to the 50mm face of the batten that will be in contact with the panel. Locate batten A with its rear edge 16mm in from the rear edge of the side panel and 50mm down from the top edge as shown in Fig. 3.

Locate batten B with its front edge 16mm back from the doorway (289mm in from the rear edge of the panel) and 50mm down from the top of the panel. Locate batten C with its front end 16mm in from the front edge of the panel and its top edge 25mm down from the top edge of the panel. Locate batten D with its front edge 16mm in from the front edge of the panel and so that its top end is in contact with the underside of batten C. Locate batten E approximately centrally between battens A and D so that its bottom edge is flush with the bottom of the panel.

The height of the seat can be set by varying the position of batten F

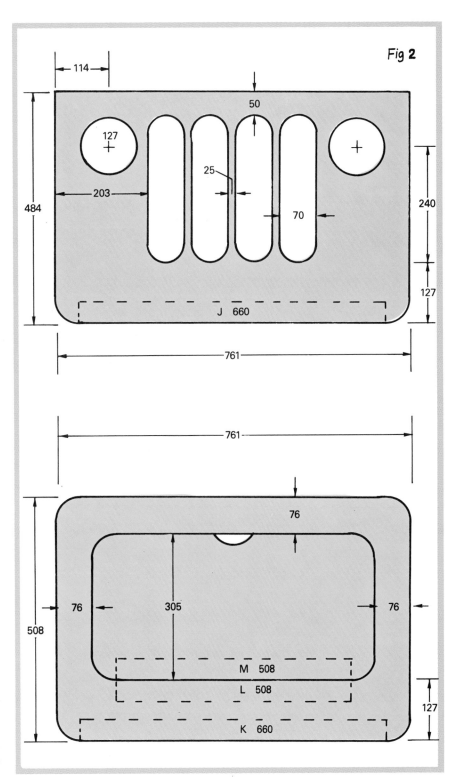

Fig 2

according to the size of the children who will use the desk, but the top edge must be at least 25mm down from the bottom edge of the doorway, and there must be a gap of 16mm between the back of batten F and the front face of batten B. Repeat this process on the other side, remembering to fix batten F at the same level on both sides so that the seat is level. Fix battens G and H centrally to the underside of the seat, 50mm in from either end as shown on the exploded diagram on the right.

Fix battens J and K centrally and flush with the bottom of the radiator and boot panels.

Fix battens L and M centrally to the boot and the boot panel and flush with edge of the boot lid aperture and the boot lid respectively.

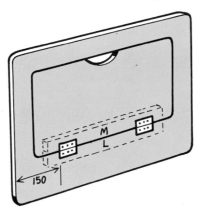

Fix batten N to the underside of the bonnet lid so that its front edge is 125mm in from the back of the panel.

Mark the centre of the screw holes for the bonnet and boot and screw on the hinges with short screws in the usual way.

On the front and rear edges of the

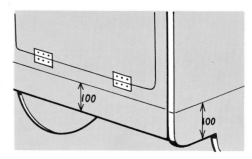

side panel, mark lines 100mm up from the bottom of the panel to guide you during assembly. Then, on the boot panels draw a line across the outside face, 100mm up from the bottom of the panel.

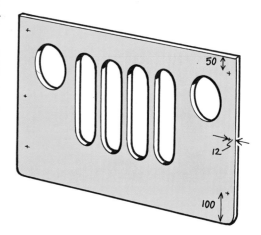

Finally, drill a series of 4mm holes 12mm in from the edge of the radiator, boot, bonnet and seat panels for assembly purposes.

Assembly

Get your helper to hold one side of the Jeep upright. Position the boot panel so that the lines you marked on earlier are level and then screw through the panel into batten A. Repeat the process with the other side, and the unit will now stand up by itself. The top and bottom of the boot panel should be level with the

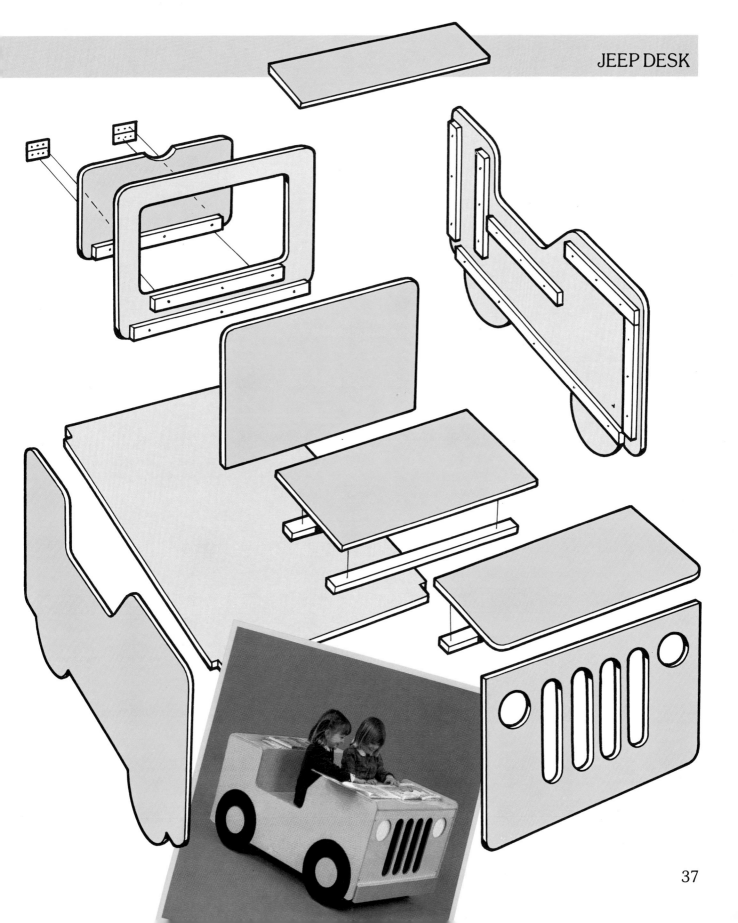

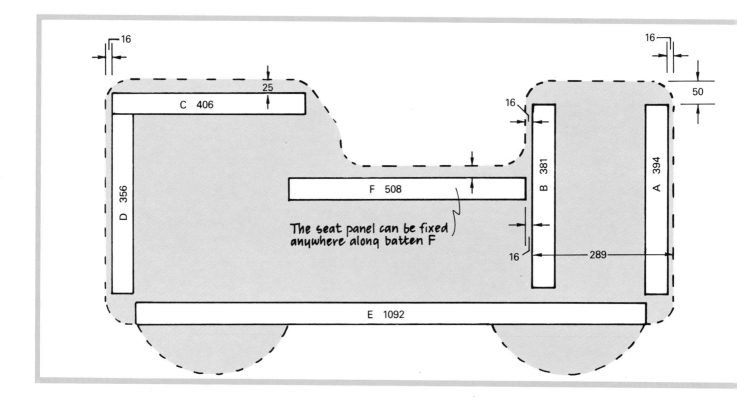

The seat panel can be fixed anywhere along batten F

top and bottom of the side panel so make this check at each corner before you go on any further.

Now position the radiator panel so that the top of the panel is level with top of batten C at each side and so that its front edge is level with the front edges of the side panels. Screw the radiator into place.

Floor panel
Measure the distance between the inside face of the radiator panel and the inside face of the boot panel. That will be the overall length of your floor panel. So cut a piece this length by 761mm or 611mm wide and cut out the corners to allow for the battens. Drill three or four 4mm diameter holes along each side 12mm in from the edge.

Pull the front end of the Jeep apart slightly so that you can slide the floor panel in until it sits on batten K at the back. Then replace the radiator panel. The base should now sit on batten J. Pull the two side panels together in the middle so that there is no gap between the edges of the base and the inside faces of the side panels. Screw the base to battens E, K and J.

Slide the seat-back down between battens B and F and block it up underneath until its top edge is level with the tops of the side panels. Screw through the seat back into battens B. Sand off the edges if the panel will not go into place easily. The shelf can now be positioned between the seat-back and the boot panel where it will sit on top of bat-

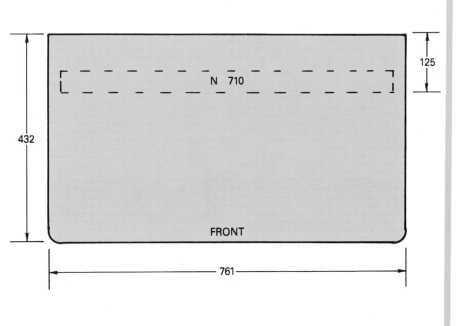

N 710

125

432

FRONT

761

tens A and B. The seat itself is intended to slide backwards and forwards on top of battens F to allow a limited amount of adjustment. So sit the driver in place and screw the seat down in the most comfortable position and also screw on the bonnet.

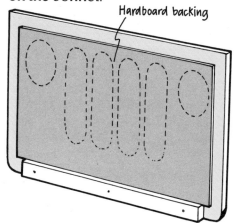

Hardboard backing

Cut a piece of hardboard, ply or chipboard 430mm × 50mm less than the width of the front panel. Lay this under the radiator panel so that it is positioned centrally and in contact with the batten J. Mark the shapes of the headlamps and grill and paint them in.

Painting

The Jeep is now ready for painting. You can finish it as a normal car, or in some sort of khaki or camouflage like a real jeep. If you decide to go for an army-type finish, there are various touches you could add like serial numbers down the side and the national insignia.

When the radiator panel has been painted, the hardboard can be glued and pinned to the back of it.

Caravan Playhouse

The Caravan Playhouse is big and strong, so you can move it around the garden like the real thing.

The Caravan Playhouse is a big, strong structure for use outside in the garden or maybe alongside the family caravan in the drive. It must be made out of exterior grade plywood because chipboard will simply not stand up to the kind of use that the Caravan is designed for.

Unlike most of the other projects in this book, the Caravan has a separate chassis made of battens so that the main structure stands up clear of the ground. This is important if you intend to park on the lawn because the grass will only be damaged in the small areas around the wheels, and you will not be left with a large area of grass that has gone yellow as you would with the other projects that sit close to the ground. Nevertheless you will always have to sit the wheels on small pieces of paving stone to prevent them sinking down into the earth.

It follows that the basic plan here can be strengthened still further during the building process. You could nail and glue a small block of wood to each corner in the chassis to brace the corners and prevent them moving at all. You could fit an extra hinge to the door so that it just cannot be pulled off. The floor could be strengthened with extra battens and finally you could pin and glue battens or pieces of quadrant moulding into the angle between the roof and the sides so that there is no tendency for the main structure to move from side to side.

But first of all, you have to decide which way you want the caravan to face and on which side you want the door. If you want it to face right to left – as in the photograph – you will need to cut out the side panels as they appear in Fig.1 and Fig.2, otherwise you will have to reverse these two plans. All the other panels stay the same whichever way round you build the caravan.

Marking Out

Mark out the side without the door in it first, remembering to work on the rougher, inside face of the sheet. When you are marking out the apertures, draw the lines to the dimensions given so that you start

Materials

5 sheets 2440mm × 1220mm 9mm exterior grade plywood
1 sheet 2440mm × 1220mm 6mm exterior grade plywood

Battens

Cut from 25mm × 100mm PAR
2 × 762mm   J,K

Cut from 25mm × 50mm PAR
2 × 1118mm   A
2 × 610mm   B
2 × 279mm   C
2 × 267mm   D
2 × 2254mm   E
2 × 1170mm   F,G,H,L
2 × 1168mm   M,N
2 × 813mm   P,Q
2 × 1981mm   R

Say 18m to allow for off-cuts.
20 50mm no.10 countersunk screws.
2 or 3 75mm rustproof hinges
100 panhead screws 25mm no.8.
12 50mm × 6mm diameter nuts, bolts, washers.
10 65mm nuts, bolts, washers.

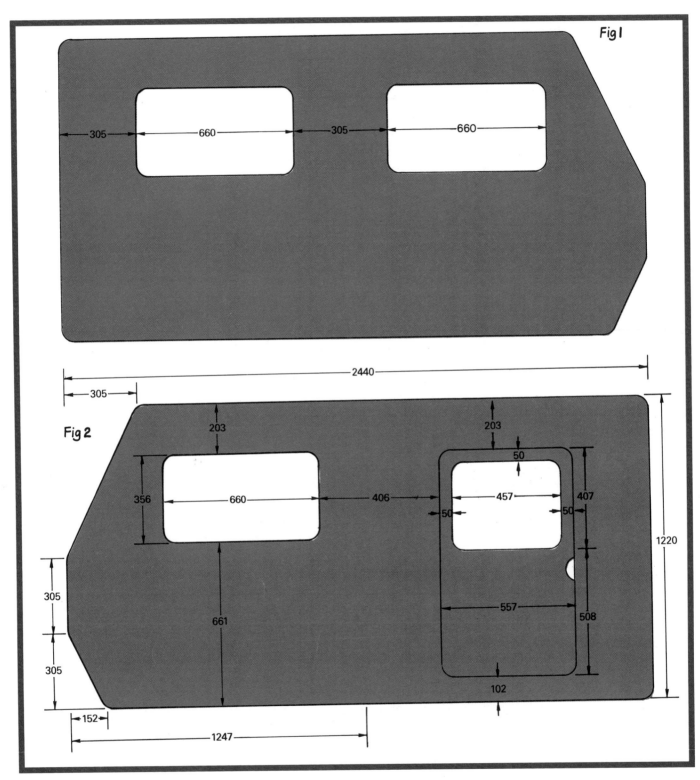

Fig 1

Fig 2

off with sharp corners. Then round the corners off by joining up the lines with a radius taken from the edge of a coin or a suitable tin. An aerosol tin has a diameter of about 65mm but anything close to that size will do. The actual radius of the corners is not critical.

Before you do anything else, mark out a line 25mm down from the top of the panel at the back sloping to 50mm down from the top of the side panel at the front end. This is the line for the top of batten R which will otherwise be difficult to locate once the panel has been cut out! Once the first side panel has been cut out, you can use it as a pattern to mark out the other side since the top of the 2nd window is in exactly the same place as the top of the door.

Drill a 9mm diameter hole close to the inside edge of each aperture to start your sawing except for the door where you can drill the hole in the finger grip.

Mark out the end panels as shown in Fig.3, on one sheet of plywood. Mark out one wheel and mudguard in the aperture of the rear window as shown below, then cut out the rear panel, the aperture

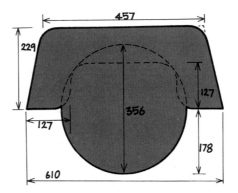

and the wheel/mudguard. Then use the wheel/mudguard you have just cut out as a pattern for the other one. Mark it out in the aperture of the window in the top front panel. Then cut out the top front panel, the aperture and the second wheel/mudguard. Cut out the middle front panel and the lower front panel, apart from the notches which have to be cut later.

From your 6mm sheet of ply cut a piece 2134mm long for the roof. For the base, cut a piece 2254mm long from a sheet of 9mm plywood. Both of these panels should be cut the full width of the sheet.

Battens
Cut battens to the sizes shown at the beginning of this section bearing in

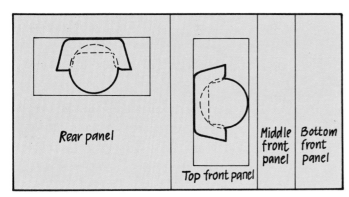

Rear panel

Top front panel
Middle front panel | Bottom front panel

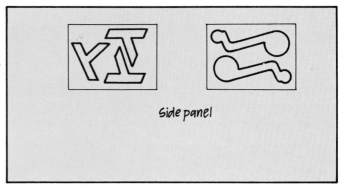

Side panel

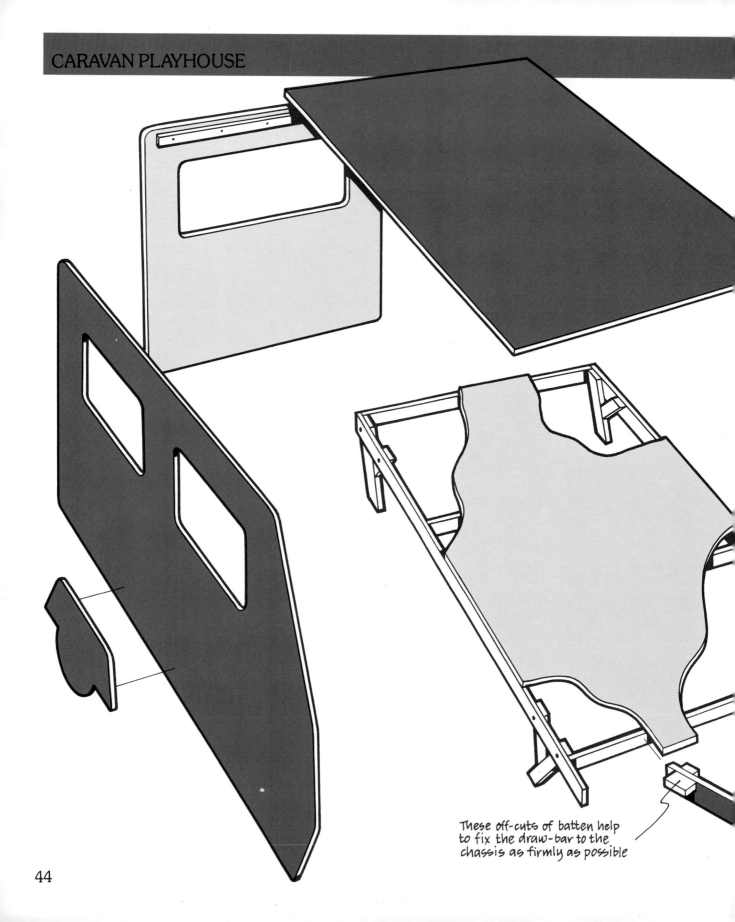

These off-cuts of batten help to fix the draw-bar to the chassis as firmly as possible

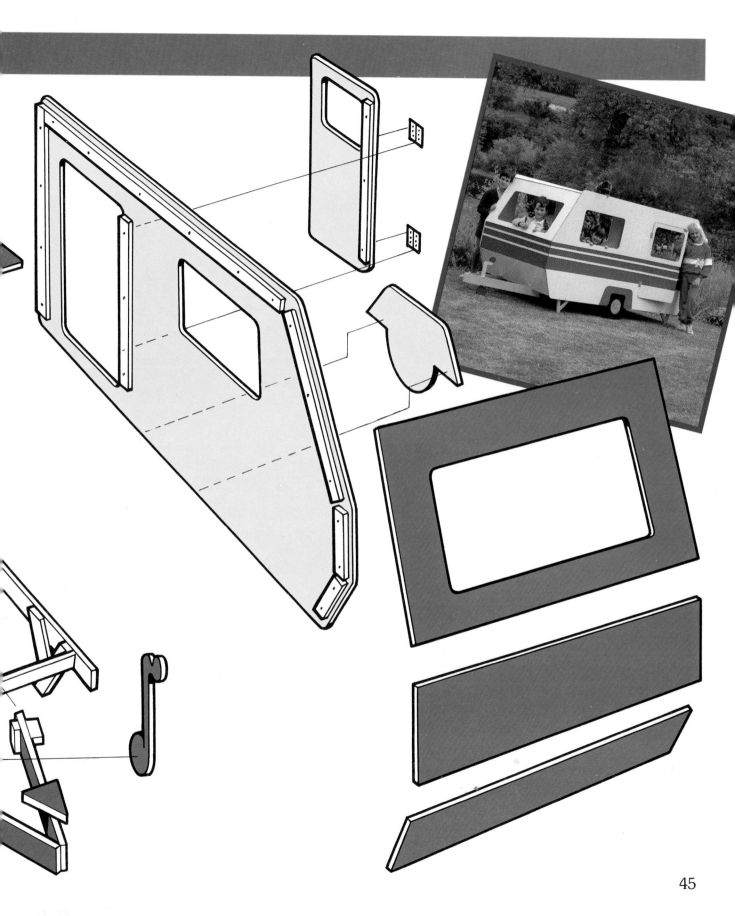

mind that two different sizes of batten are used in this project. Sand and bevel the edges as necessary.

Drill a series of 4mm diameter holes through the 50mm face of battens A, B, C, D, N, M at 300mm or so intervals. Apply adhesive to the 50mm face that will be in contact with the side panel, one batten at a time. Fix the battens for the side panel with no door in it first as shown on Fig.5, bearing in mind that this diagram shows the side looking outwards from inside the body of the caravan.

Locate batten A so that its top corner is on the sloping line that you drew earlier and so that its rear edge is 38mm in from the edge of the

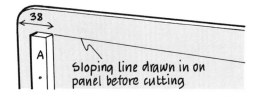

panel. Screw down. Locate batten B so that its top corner is on the sloping line and so that its front edge is 25mm in from the front edge of the panel. Screw down. Locate batten D so that its bottom corner is 50mm up from the bottom of the panel and so that its front edge is 25mm in from the front edge of the panel.

Locate batten C with its front edge 25mm back from the front edge of the side panel and approximately midway between battens B and D. Batten C should not be allowed to protrude in front of a line extended from the front of battens B or D. Locate batten R more or less centrally between battens A and B

and in such a way that its top edge is on the sloping line. Repeat this procedure for the other side.

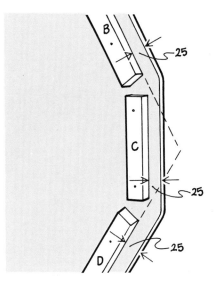

For a really weatherproof door arrangement, leave fitting the door until later. Otherwise, fix batten P to the inside face of the door with the front edge of the batten flush with the front edge of the door and the bottom of the batten 50mm up from the bottom of the door. Fix batten Q to the door frame with its rear edge flush with the door aperture and its bottom end 152mm up from the bottom of the panel.

Turn the panel and door over to fix the hinges. It would be advisable to put a couple of bits of batten under the door so that it is level with the rest of the panel. Mark on the door and door frames a line 100mm up from the bottom of the door to show the position of the bottom of the lower hinge. Then mark another line 915mm up from the bottom of the panel to show the position of the top of the upper door hinge.

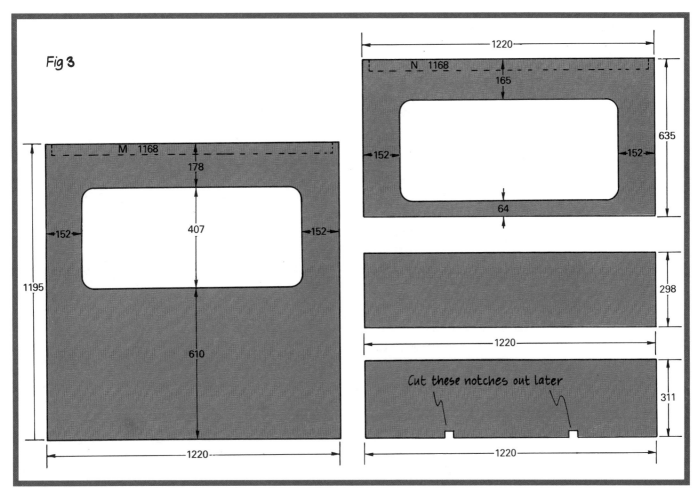

Fig 3

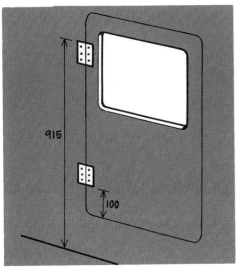

Position the hinge so that the centre of the hinge is over the edge of the aperture. Mark the centre of the screw holes on the door frame and make starter holes with a nail or bradawl. Drill 2mm diameter holes to a depth of about 12mm. Screw on the hinges. Make sure that the door is flush with the side of the caravan and that the gap at the top and the bottom of the door is more or less equal. Mark, tap and drill the screw holes for one hinge and check how the door fits. If it is alright, fix the remaining hinges into place.

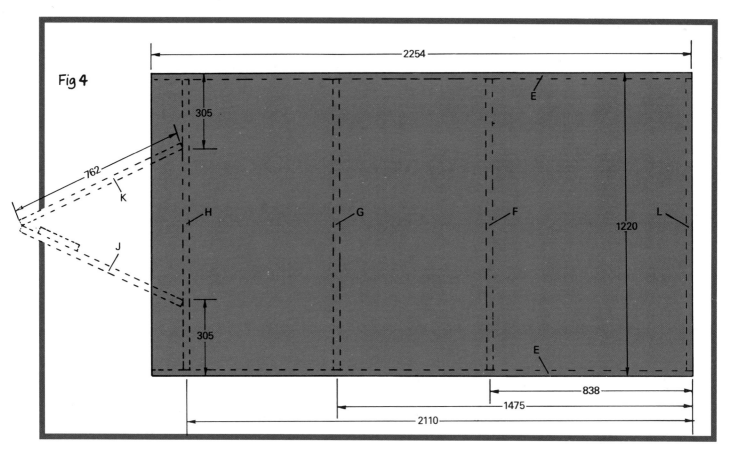

Fig 4

Chassis

You can now transfer your attention to the chassis of the caravan.

Mitre the front end of battens E as shown here and trim the transverse battens F, G, H and L to a length equal to the width of the floor less the thickness of the two battens E.

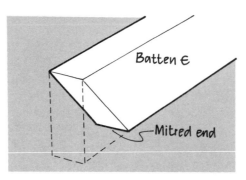

Batten E

Mitred end

Due to the planing process, battens E will be less than 25mm thick by a varying amount, so it is not possible to give a precise dimension for the transverse battens in advance.

Drill a series of 4mm diameter holes in the floor as shown in Fig.6. Drill a row of 4mm diameter holes through the 50mm face of the battens E spaced as shown on Fig.4 and countersink the holes on the outside. Apply adhesive to battens E and position these under the floor so that they are flush with the edges. Screw through floor into battens E.

Turn the assembly over now so that the battens E are uppermost. Apply adhesive to the edge of battens F, G, H and L, then position them so that the centre of each batten lines up with a pair of the holes drilled in batten E, or, in the case of batten L, so that it is flush with the rear edge of the floor panel.

Use 50mm countersunk screws to screw through battens E into the ends of battens F, G, H and L. Turn the assembly over again and screw through the floor into battens F, G, H and L. Brace this assembly with blocks of wood glued and pinned into the corners of the battens to make a really good job of it.

Cut four corner steadies from 18mm plywood or cut eight of them

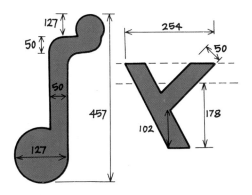

from 9mm ply offcuts as shown on the cutting diagram earlier and glue them together in pairs. Round off all the edges. Cut the jockey wheel from 18mm ply or 2 from 9mm ply glued together. Turn the floor assembly over again so that the battens are uppermost.

Position the draw-bar so that the corners of the 100mm × 25mm battens are 305mm in from the outer edges of the panel at the point where they touch batten H. Mark round the draw-bar batten on the underside of the floor. Now drill two

4mm diameter holes in the floor at each side so you can screw the draw-bar into place.

Get an assistant to hold the draw-bar assembly in place on the floor panel while you screw up through the floor into the battens through the holes that you have just drilled. Make sure that the ends of the draw-bar battens are correctly

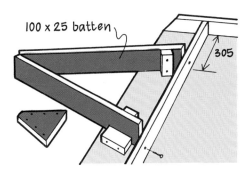

100 x 25 batten

305

placed 305mm in from the outer edge of the floor panel. Tighten the screws right up. Drill a hole through batten H just into the ends of the draw-bar battens and use a 50mm screw to screw through into the draw-bar battens. Do not drill this hole out to the full depth. Screw into the draw-bar battens carefully or there is a danger that you will split the wood. Glue and pin small blocks of wood in the angle between the draw-bar battens and the floor attachment of the draw-bar to the floor.

Locate the corner steadies against the inside of battens E so that the front pair are touching the rear face of batten H and the rear pair are touching the front face of batten L. The legs should point inwards towards the middle of the caravan. Drill 6mm diameter holes

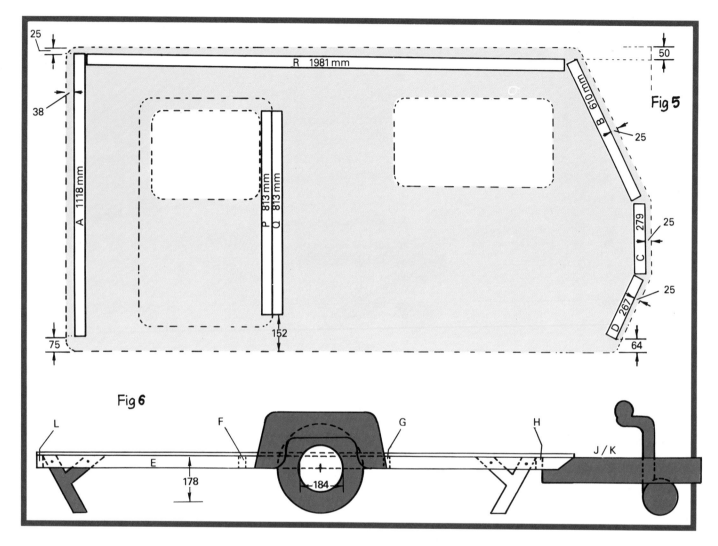

Fig 5

Fig 6

through battens E and through the corner steadies. Countersink the outside of the holes in battens E. Now insert your 65mm × 6mm countersunk bolts through the holes, slip the washer and nut onto the thread and tighten until the head is flush with the surface.

Being careful not to trip over the draw-bar, cut a piece of ply 150mm × 300mm and lay it over the front of the draw-bar. Mark off flush with the outside of the draw-bar and cut to shape. Drill three 4mm diameter holes along each side of the plywood so that you can screw the ply to the top of the draw-bar. With your electric sander or rasp, flatten off the front of the draw-bar battens, flush with the plywood. Fix the jockey wheel to the draw-bar with two 50mm × 6mm nuts and bolts, making sure that draw-bar and floor are horizontal. Finally, drill a series of 6mm diameter holes in each side panel as shown above right.

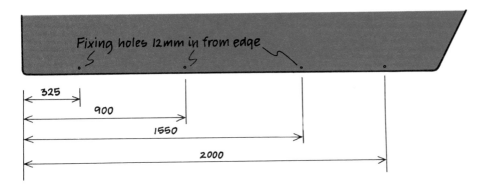

Fixing holes 12mm in from edge

325
900
1550
2000

Assembly

You will almost certainly need some assistance to fix the side panels in place. Get one helper to hold the side panel up while you fix it to batten E with panel pins in such a way that the bottom of the panel is flush with the bottom of batten E and the back of the floor is flush with the rear edge of batten A. Once it is firmly in position and while it is still being steadied by your assistant, drill through the 6mm holes in the side panel and all the way through the batten E. Insert your 6mm nuts and bolts with a washer on the inside face of batten E and tighten them up.

Once the nuts and bolts are tight, ask your second assistant to hold the other side in place while you repeat the procedure.

Now drill a row of 4mm diameter holes in the rear panel so you can screw it into place. Position the rear panel so that its top edge is level with the top of battens A and screw through the panel into battens A and batten L. The rear panel will brace the two sides so your assistants can now let go of them.

Drill a series of 4mm diameter holes 12mm in from the edge of the

three front panels. Position the top front panel so that its top edge is level with the sloping lines on the side panels and screw through into

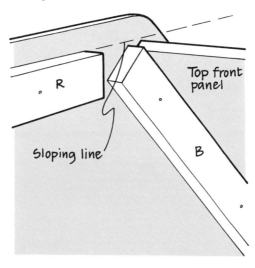

R

Top front panel

Sloping line

B

battens B. Position the front middle panel so that its top edge is tight up against the front panel and screw through into battens C.

The bottom front panel has to have two notches cut in its bottom edge where it fits over the draw-bar battens. Position the bottom front panel so that it is sitting on the draw-bar and push the bottom edge back until it is touching the front of the floor. Then mark where you need to cut the notches. You will

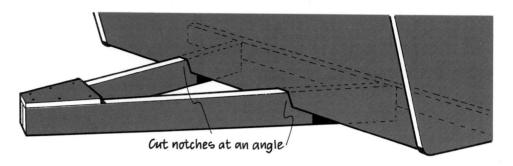

Cut notches at an angle

observe that they have to be cut at an angle following the direction of the draw-bar battens. The height of the notch is a matter of trial and error. So cut away a little at a time until the top edge of the panel is a snug fit under the bottom edge of the middle front panel.

Drill a series of 4mm diameter holes down the long edges of the roof 12mm in from the edge and at 450mm or so intervals. Lift the roof into place so that there is an equal overhang beyond at front and rear. Then ask your assistant to push the sides together so that there is no gap between the edges of the roof and the inside faces of the side panels and screw down through the roof into battens R. Now drill three 4mm diameter holes along the front and back edges into battens M and N and screw down through the roof into the battens once more.

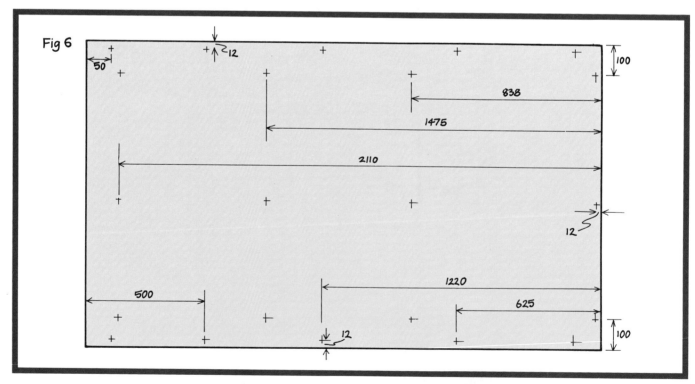

Fig 6

Weatherproofing

Providing you have used exterior grade materials and an exterior paint system, the caravan will stand up well to the weather. However, if you want to make it completely waterproof, you will need to seal all the joints with a waterproof mastic, glaze the windows and create a proper door frame. If you wish to do this, the unit should first be sealed with mastic and then painted fully assembled. Make sure you use a primer/undercoat which will adhere to the mastic properly.

The easiest way to glaze the windows is to obtain some rectangular pieces of 4mm perspex, 25mm bigger all round than the window apertures.

These can either be pop-riveted from the inside or bolted from the outside using 18mm × 4mm nuts and bolts. You can then run a small fillet of mastic round the window frame.

If you want to build a weatherproof version, you will also need to create a proper door frame. This frame can be glued and screwed with 15mm countersunk screws to the inside of the side panel so that it protrudes into the doorway by 25mm all the way round.

Since you will have to leave out the battens for the hinge screws to go into, you will have to use screws which penetrate less than 9mm into the door and less than 18mm into the doorframes, so you would be well advised to use three hinges rather than two, and to use plastic inserts for the screws to bite into.

Once the unit is painted, you could, as an added refinement, put a strip of self-adhesive draught excluder round the frame to keep the dust out. You can put any lock, clamp or catch of your choice on the door and door frame to keep it closed. The simplest arrangement will probably be a back-door-type lock and handle fitted to the outside acting on the door frame.

Finishing

Paint the wheels and mudguards next which is best done while they are lying on the bench. Make sure that each colour is completely dry before you paint on an adjoining or an overlapping one. When they are painted, they can be fixed to the side panels so that the bottom of the mudguard is flush with the bottom of the panel. Use a couple of pan-head screws drilled through into battens E. The centre line of the wheel should be in the position shown in Fig.2.

The ultimate outfit for ambitious kids is a Jeep desk with a Caravan hitched up behind it and all painted in the same colours.

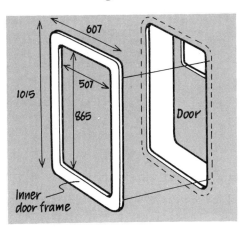

607
1015
507
865
Door
Inner door frame

Truck Bed

In this Truck the load is stored under the bonnet and on the roof while the driver has a bunk in the cab.

Materials

3 sheets 2440mm × 1220mm 9mm plywood.
1 sheet 2440mm × 1220mm chipboard OR 4 sheets 2440mm × 1220mm chipboard.

Battens

Cut from 25mm × 50mm PAR

2 ×	305mm	A
2 ×	419mm	B
2 ×	889mm	C
2 ×	533mm	D
2 ×	581mm	E
2 ×	484mm	F
2 ×	457mm	G
2 ×	2311mm	H
2 ×	330mm	J,K
1 ×	762mm	L
2 ×	660mm	M,P
4 ×	710mm	N,Q,R,S

19m battening with an allowance for waste.
2 75mm hinges.
100 pan head 25mm no.8 screws.

This impressive truck not only provides a snug bed for one, it also has a good deal of storage space under the bonnet where the engine used to be. And above the cab is a large, deep tray which is perfect for all the toys scooped off the floor and the bed just before bedtime.

Unlike the bunk beds described elsewhere in this book, there is no real advantage in fixing the truck to the wall. Far better to build the truck so that it is free standing, then it can be moved around to make room for other activities when necessary.

As in the case of the other vehicle beds, the headlights in the front of the truck could be cut-out and small lights fitted behind to illuminate the whole of the bedroom or to act as a night light. Older children might also appreciate a light inside the cab to act as a reading lamp without the need of a bedside table to get in the way of things.

Before you start, you will need to decide which way round you want the truck to face, bearing in mind that you will be marking out on the inside, rougher face of the plywood. So, if you want the rig to face left to right as it does in the photograph, you will need to cut out the side panels as they appear in Figs.1 and

2. On the other hand, if you want the door to face the other direction, you must mark the sides out in the reverse way. The remainder of the panels are not affected by the way you face the truck. Of course there is no reason why you cannot have a door in both sides.

Marking Out

Mark out the side without the door first. When this has been cut out, you can use it as a pattern for the other side since the front window on that side is in exactly the same place as the window in the door.

When you mark the apertures on to the sheets, you will find that the dimensions given simply refer to straight lines. So the corners will come up as right angles when you draw all the lines in. You can round off the corners by fitting the base of an aerosol can into the angle so that it joins up each side smoothly, without any bumps or ripples. Then draw round the base of the can to get the smooth rounded line that you are after.

Drill a 9mm diameter hole, to start your cut, close to the inside edges of the apertures except in the case of the door, where you can drill in the finger hole.

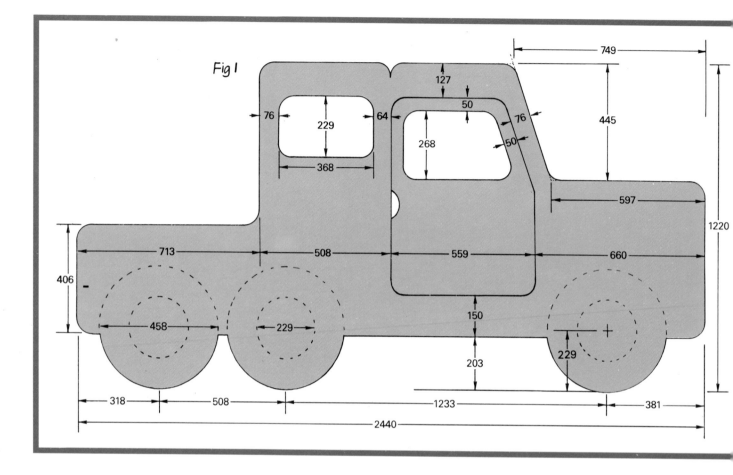

Fig I

Mark and cut out the rear, bonnet, roof, and radiator panels according to Figs.3 and 4. The diameter of the headlamps does not have to be exactly 127mm, so long as its rim is at least 25mm down from the top edge of the panel and at least 38mm in from the side. The rounded corners on the bonnet lid should be drawn round a 10p coin similar to the way you marked the corners of the apertures in order to get a smooth regular curve.

For the time being just cut a 762mm × 500mm panel for the windscreen. You will have to work out the size for this panel later.

Battens

Cut battens to the lengths shown at the beginning of this section. Sand and bevel the edges and corners and round off one end of battens A. Drill a series of 4mm diameter holes through the middle of the 50mm face of the battens, one hole 50mm in from either end and the others at 300mm – 450mm intervals, with the exception of battens G and H where the holes must be 25mm from each end.

Take one batten and one panel at a time. Apply adhesive to the 50mm face of the batten that will be in contact with the panel (25mm face in

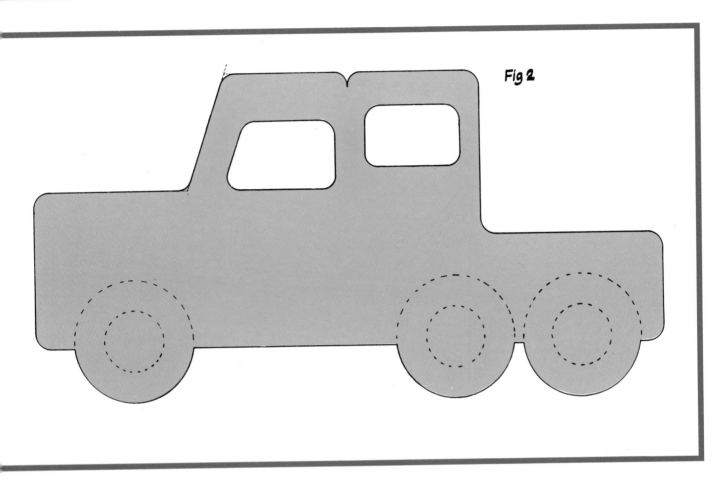

Fig 2

the case of batten L). Start with the side panel without a door and locate batten A with its rear edge 13mm in from the rear edge of the side panel and its rounded end 50mm down from the top of the panel as shown in Fig.5. Screw the batten down.

Locate batten B 13mm back from the front edge of the side panel with its top corner 50mm down from the top of the side panel. Screw down. Fix batten C so that its bottom edge is flush with the top of the rear window aperture (127mm down from the top of the panel) and with its rear end 50mm in from the rear end of the panel. Fix batten D so that its

top end is level with the top edge of batten C and its rear edge flush with the edge of the panel.

Fix batten E so that its front end is 13mm back from the front edge of the panel and with its top edge 25mm down from the top of the panel. Fix batten F with its front edge 13mm back from the front edge of the panel and with its top end touching the underside of batten E. Fix batten G with its rear edge level with the rear end of batten E (594mm back from the front edge of the panel).

Fix batten H more or less centrally between battens A and F in

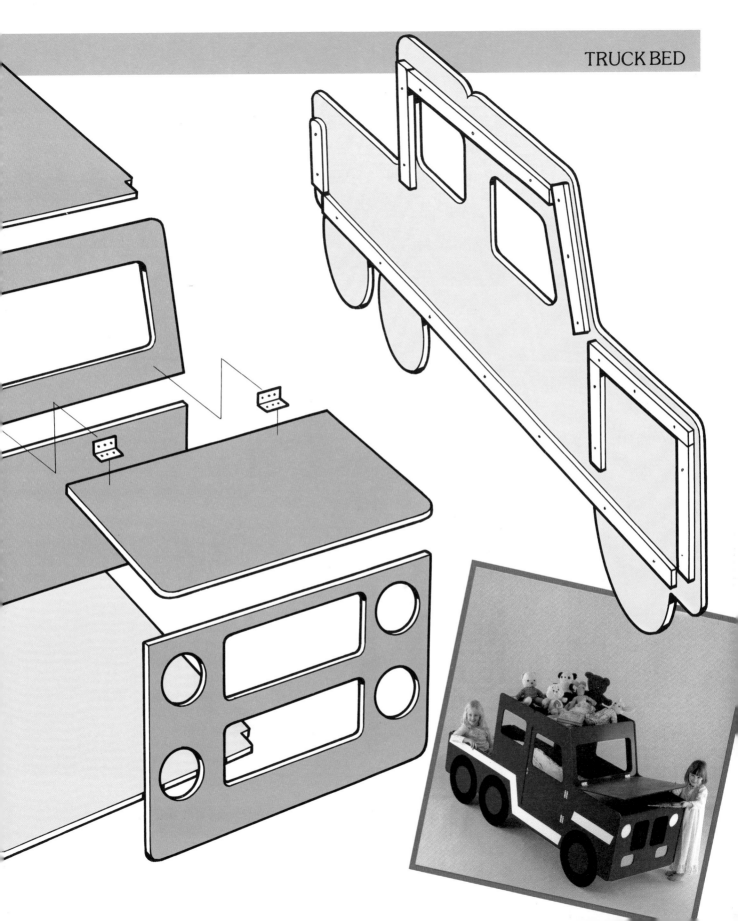

such a way that its bottom edge is flush with bottom edge of the panel.

Repeat this process for the other side and then fix the battens J and K for the door hinges. Both should have their bottom ends 200mm up from the bottom of the panel. The rear edge of batten J should be flush with the door aperture and the front edge of batten K should be flush with front edge of the door.

Turn the panel over and put a couple of batten off-cuts under the door so that it is level with the side panel. Locate the hinges as shown below and mark the centre of the screw holes on the door frame, making sure that the centre of the hinge is over the edge of the aper-

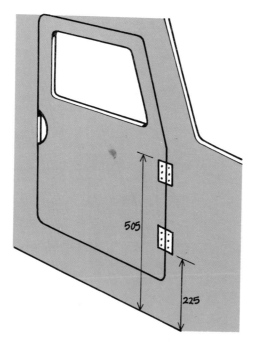

ture. Make the starter hole with a nail or bradawl. Drill 2mm diameter holes to a depth of about 12mm and screw the hinge to the door frame.

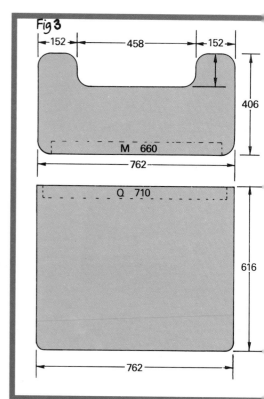

Fig 3

Position the door so that there is an even gap all the way round. Mark the position of the screw holes. Mark, drill, and then screw the hinges to the door.

Fix batten M centrally to the rear panel so that its bottom edge is flush with the bottom edge of the panel. Fix batten N and P in a similar way to the radiator panel. Fix batten Q to the underside of the bonnet lid panel, so that its rear edge is flush with the rear edge of the bonnet panel with 26mm clearance between the end of the batten and the edge of the panel.

Mark a line on the front and rear edge of the side panels 100mm up from the bottom edge. Again, draw lines across the outside face of the

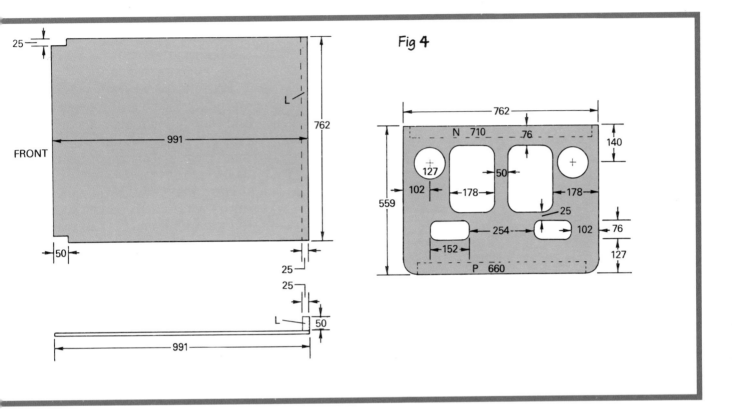

Fig 4

radiator panel and the rear panel 100mm up from the bottom edge and drill a series of 4mm diameter holes in these panels for assembly purposes.

Assembly

You are now ready to begin assembly, during which time you will need some temporary assistance.

Ask your helper to hold one of the sides upright. Position the rear panel so that the marks you have just drawn 100mm up from the bottom of each panel line up and screw through the rear panel into batten A. Now do the same with the other side and the truck should stand up by itself.

Position the radiator panel so that again your marks line up and screw to batten F at each side. Measure the distance between the inside face of the radiator panel and the inside face of the rear panel. This will give you the length of the floor panel allowing for any variations in the position and the thickness of the battens. Cut this out including the notches in the corners. Drill a series of 4mm diameter holes 12mm in from the edges at 300mm – 450mm intervals for the screws.

Unscrew the radiator panel, pull the sides apart slightly and slide the floor along the tops of battens H until it is resting on the top of batten M. Replace the radiator panel. Check that everything is in square, then screw the floor down into bat-

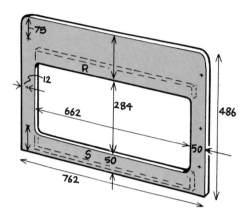

Bed down into separate panels, you can squeeze glue along the edge of the floor panel before you screw it down for extra strength.

Take the panel from which you are going to make the windscreen and slide it down against battens B until it is resting on battens E. Now mark the top of the windscreen level with the top of the side panels.

Next, mark a point on either side of the windscreen panel level with the top of battens C. This will then give you the position of the top of batten R. Cut out the windscreen opening and fix battens R and S to the inside of the panel.

Drill a series of 4mm diameter holes 12mm in from the edge of the

tens H, M and P. Make sure that the sides are well pulled together so that there is no gap between the edges of the floor and the inside faces of the side panels. If you are sure you will never want to break the Truck

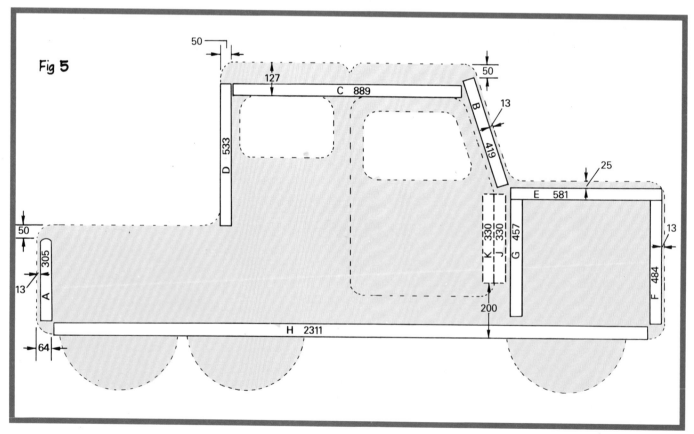

Fig 5

windscreen panel and screw it into place. Drill a series of 4mm diame-

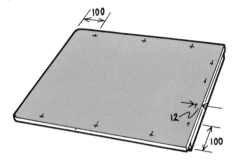

ter holes 12mm in from the rear edge and sides of the roof panel.

Apply adhesive to one of the 25mm faces of batten L. Drill and screw through the roof panel from the underside into batten L making sure that its rear edge and ends are flush with the edges of the roof panel. Place roof panel in position with batten L on top so that it forms the back lip of the tray. Make sure that the assembly is not out of square. Pulling the sides well together so that there is no gap between the edges of the roof panel and the side panels, screw down through the holes already drilled in the roof panel into battens C.

Slide the bonnet panel with the batten underneath along the top of battens E until it comes into contact with the windscreen panel. You can now position the hinges as shown allowing 100mm between the side panels and the outside end of the hinges. Mark, drill and screw through into battens Q and S.

Cut out the partition from an off-cut of chipboard. There is not enough left from cutting out the floor to make a panel big enough to run from floor to windscreen, so

leave a gap at the top or the bottom or better still make the partition in two sections. Drill 2 or 3 4mm diameter holes 12mm in from the edge of the partition and fix to the back of battens G. If you want to fill in the whole space with a partition, measure the distance between the floor and the windscreen along batten G and cut 2 pieces half this length × 762mm (they will measure about 250mm each).

Painting

You can paint the truck in the fairly sober way as shown in the pictures here but with the aid of some metallic paint, preferably in aerosol form, you can adopt some of the more spectacular customized paint jobs that are now on the roads or even copy one of the racing trucks.

Do not forget the number plates at the front and the back, based either on the name of whoever is occupying the bed or on the number of the family car.

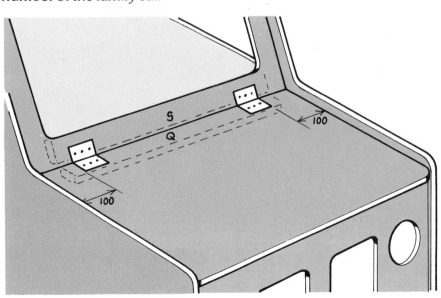

Delivery Van Bunk Beds

A ladder at the back gives access to the top bunk – you can reach the bottom one through the door.

The Delivery Van bunk bed is roughly the same size as the Camper but it is a little easier and quicker to make as it requires less cutting out and it does offer a good amount of storage under the bonnet instead of having a writing desk like the Camper.

Like the Camper, the Delivery Van has an upper and lower deck, each providing a bed so you ought to consider fixing the Delivery Van to the wall for stability instead of having it free standing. The big advantage of the Delivery Van is that it offers slightly easier access to the lower bunk for really young children.

In the illustration here, the Delivery Van is painted in a traditional livery but with imagination and several tins of paint, you could convert this workaday vehicle into a racing car transporter complete with suitable colour scheme and logos or even an ice cream van.

To begin with, you will need to decide which way round you want the bed to face. Bear in mind that you will be marking out on the rougher inside face. So, if you want the bed to face right to left as it does in the photograph you will need to cut out the side panels as shown in Figs.1 and 2. Otherwise these two plans will have to be reversed.

The front panels are symmetrical, so are not affected by the way the van faces, but the rear panel is not. If the bed is to stand against a wall the steps in the rear panel should be nearest the wall. So if the bed faces right to left, you will need to mark and cut out the rear panel (on the inside face) as it appears in Fig.3, otherwise this plan will need to be reversed as well.

Marking Out

Start by marking and cutting out the side panel with the doorway. When the panel is cut out, you can use it as a pattern for the other side, making the necessary adjustments so that you have a window rather than a doorway against the wall. On the other hand, there is nothing to stop you having a doorway on both sides, in which case make two panels using Fig.1 as a pattern but arranged so that the smooth side of both sheets faces outwards.

Materials.

3 sheets 2440mm × 1220mm 9mm plywood PLUS
2 sheets 2440mm × 1220mm chipboard OR
5 sheets 2440mm × 1220mm chipboard.

Battens

Cut from 25mm × 50mm PAR

2 ×	1016mm	A
2 ×	508mm	B
2 ×	457mm	C
2 ×	445mm	D
2 ×	406mm	E
2 ×	1702mm	F
2 ×	2311mm	G
5 ×	864mm	H,K,L,M,N
2 ×	813mm	J,P

21m of battening allowing for waste.
100 panhead 25mm no. 8 screws.
2 75mm hinges.

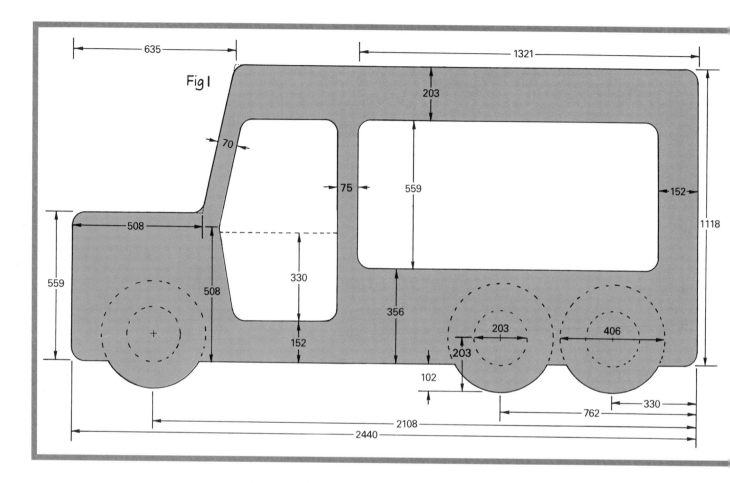

Fig I

As with all the other vehicle projects, the corners of the openings in the sides must be rounded off for strength. The dimensions shown on the plan should be marked on to the sheets so that the corners are roughly at right angles. You then mark in the rounded corners by placing the base of an aerosol can or a similar object in the angle of the corner, though it needs a bit of care to avoid any sort of bump in the line between the curve and the straight part of the aperture. As for the corners of the bonnet panel, these should be drawn round a 10p coin to give you a much tighter radius.

Cut out the rear panel, the radiator panel and the bonnet panel from your third sheet of ply. The partition can be cut from the material cut-out of one of the rear apertures in the side panel.

It is not essential to make the diameter of the headlamps exactly 127mm, providing their rims are at least 38mm in from the outside edge of the radiator panel and at least 50mm down from the top edge of the rear panel.

For the time being just cut a rectangular panel 914mm × 650mm for the windscreen and cut out the window aperture.

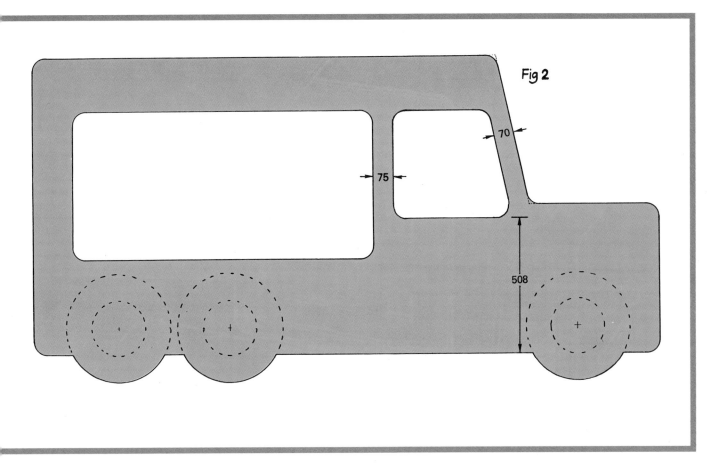

Fig 2

Battens

Cut the battens to the lengths shown at the beginning of this section. Round one end of battens A and B. Sand and slightly bevel the edges and corners of the rest.

Drill a series of 4mm diameter holes through the centre of the 50mm face of the battens, one hole 50mm in from either end and the rest spaced at 300mm – 450mm intervals. Make sure that every batten has at least three holes in it. Screw on the battens one at a time and complete one panel before you go on to the next. Apply the PVA adhesive to the 50mm face of the

batten which will touch the panel.

Position batten A with its top end 50mm down from the top edge of the panel and with its rear face 13mm in from the rear edge of the panel. Screw down. Fix batten B so that the rounded end is 50mm down from the top edge of the side panel, and with its front face 13mm in from the front edge of the side panel. Fix batten C with its top end 25mm down from the top of the panel and its front face 13mm in from the front of the panel.

Draw a line which is a continuation downwards of the front edge of batten B. Now fix batten D so that

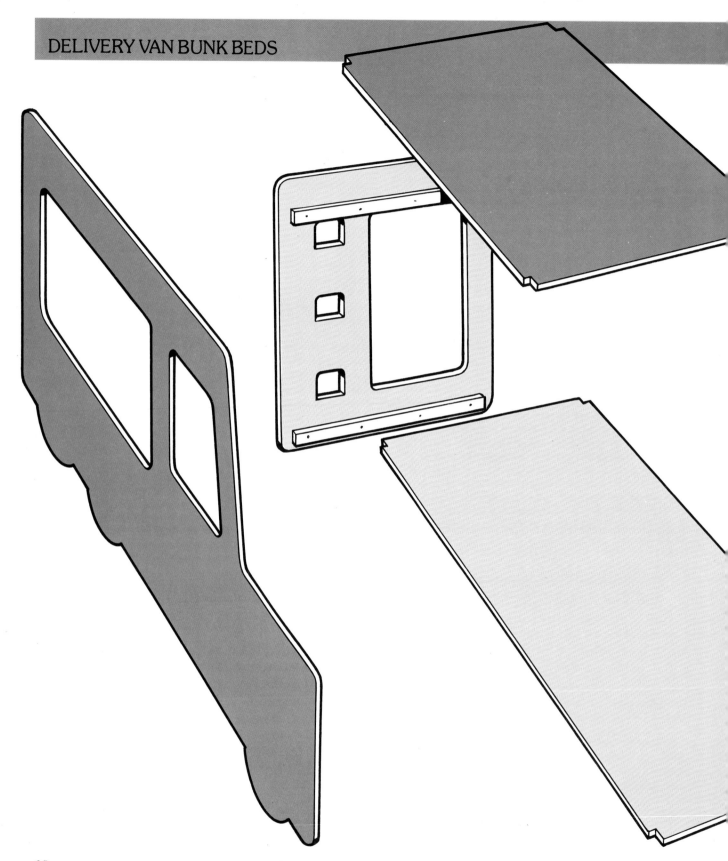

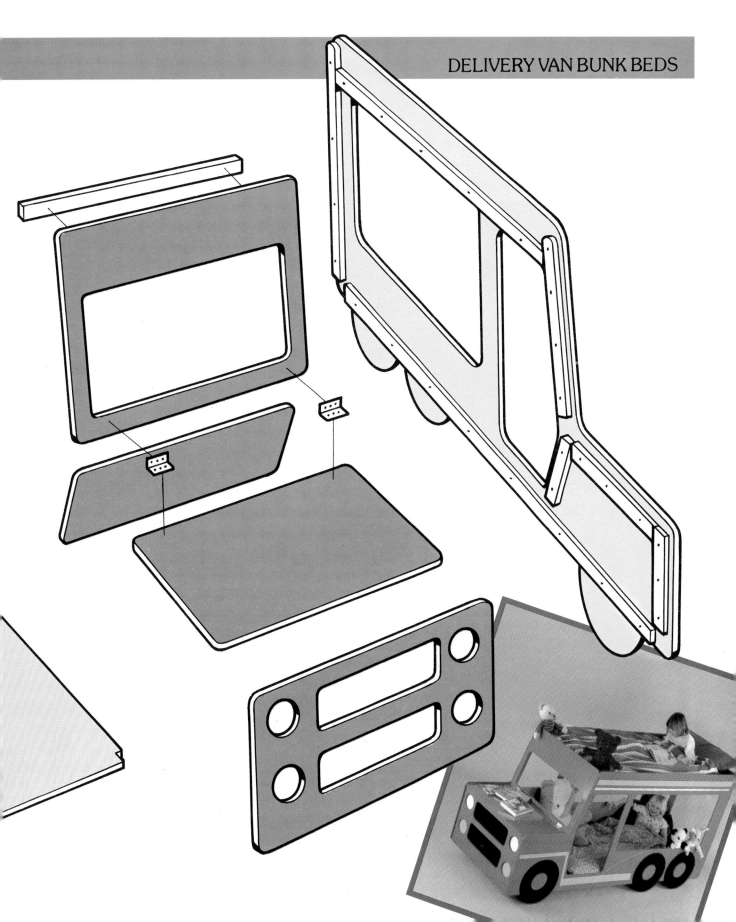

its top edge is 25mm down from the edge of the panel and so that its top rear corner touches the line you have just drawn at point W.

Next, mark a point 600mm back from the front edge of the side panel, point X. Then draw a line between point W and point X. Fix batten E in place so that its rear edge is on the line WX and so that its top is in contact with the bottom rear corner of batten D.

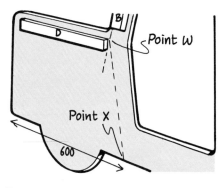

Fix batten F approximately centrally between battens A and B so that its underside is flush with the top of the apertures, 203mm down from the top edge of the panel. Fix batten G approximately midway between battens A and C so that its underside is flush with the bottom of the panel.

Fix batten H to the inside face of the rear panel, so that its underside is flush with the top of the aperture (203mm down from the top edge of the panel) but clear of the step. There should be a gap of about 25mm at each end of the batten.

Fix batten J to the inside of the rear panel so that its underside is flush with the bottom of the panel and with a space of about 50mm at either end.

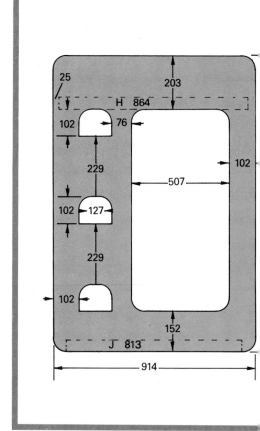

Fix battens N and P flush with the top and bottom respectively of the radiator panel as shown in Fig.4.

Fix batten K to the underside of the bonnet panel so that its rear edge is flush with the rear edge of the panel and with a gap of about 25mm at each end.

Assembly
Mark a point on the front and rear edge of the side panels 100mm up from the bottom of the panel. Draw a line on the outside faces of the radiator and rear panels 100mm up from the bottom of the panel. Drill a

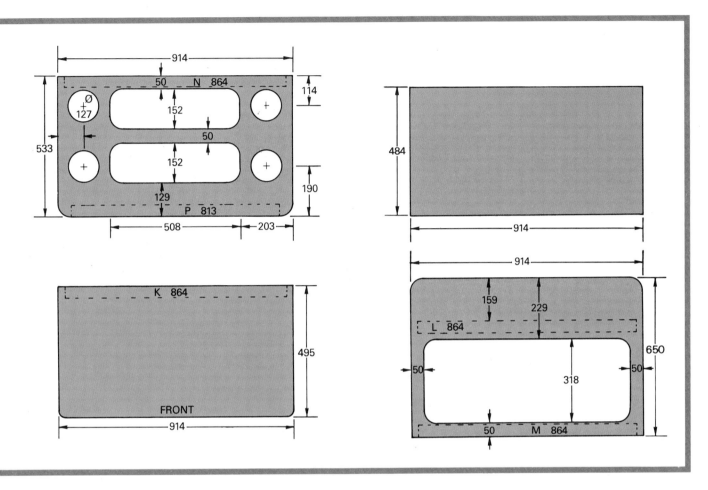

series of 4mm diameter holes 12mm in from the edge of the rear and radiator panels.

Get your helper to hold one of the side panels vertical while you take the rear panel, line up your

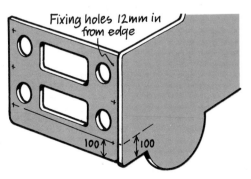

Fixing holes 12mm in from edge

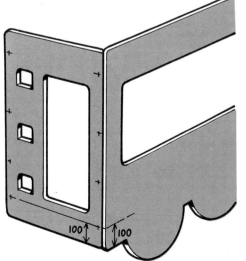

71

marks and screw through into batten A. Repeat this procedure for the other side. The Delivery Van should now stand up by itself.

Position the radiator panel so that the marks line up and screw through into battens C.

Now measure the distance between the inside face of the radiator panel and the inside face of the rear panel. This will give you the length of the floor panel, allowing for any variation in the thickness of the battens. Cut this out including the corner notches to clear the battens.

Drill a series of 4mm diameter holes 12mm in from the edges of the floor panel at 300mm – 450mm intervals. Remove the radiator panel. Pull the front of the side panels apart slightly and slide the floor in along the tops of battens G

until it is resting on batten J. Squeeze a line of woodworking adhesive between the side of the Van and the edge of the floor panel if you want to build this unit really strongly. Screw the radiator panel back in. Push the side panels together so that there is no gap between the edges of the floor panel and the inside faces of the side panels. Screw through the floor into battens G, J and P.

Position the 914mm × 650mm windscreen panel so that it is tight up against battens B with its bottom edge resting on battens D. Mark a point on either side of the inside face of the windscreen panel level with the top of battens F and another level with the top of the side panels. These will now give you the position of the top of batten L and

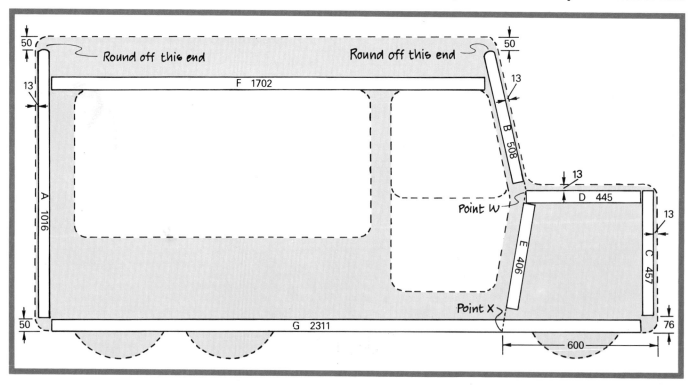

the top of the windscreen panel respectively. Cut out the panel and fix battens L and M to the inside face of the windscreen as in Fig.4.

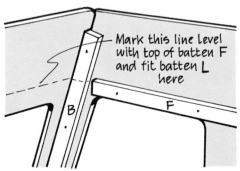

Mark this line level with top of batten F and fit batten L here

Drill a series of 4mm diameter holes 12mm in from the outside edge of the windscreen panel and screw through into battens B. Sit the bonnet panel on top of battens D and slide it back until its rear edge touches the windscreen panel. Position the hinges with their outer edges 100mm in from the outer edge of the panel and mark the centre of the screw holes on the bonnet and windscreen panels. Make guide holes with a nail or bradawl and drill 2mm diameter holes to a depth of about 12mm. Screw on the hinges.

Measure the distance along the top of battens F between the inside face of the windscreen panel and inside face of the rear panel. This

will give you the length of the upper floor. Cut out this panel including the corner notches and drill a series of 4mm diameter holes at 300mm – 450mm intervals 12mm in from the edges. Lay the upper floor panel on top of battens F, H and L. Ask your assistant to make sure that the side panels are well pushed together so that there is no gap between the edge of the floor and the side panels, and screw down into the battens. Again you can glue this panel in place for extra strength if you wish.

Finishing

Cut a piece of scrap hardboard, plywood or chipboard 430mm × 864mm. Position this on the underside of the radiator panel and mark out the grill and headlamps.

You can now paint in the colours for the headlamps and grill going 12mm or so over the shapes you have marked. When dry, glue and pin the painted panel to the inside of the radiator panel.

Paint the Van, starting with the inside and working down from the top with primer, undercoat and top coat. Allow that to harden for a couple of days and then mark on the details and paint them in in suitably flamboyant colours.

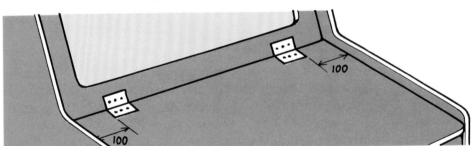

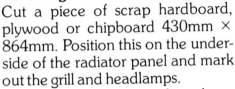

Piggy Cupboard

If these pigs had wings, they would be crazy to fly away from this beautiful cupboard.

Materials.

1 sheet 2440mm × 1220mm
9mm plywood PLUS
1 sheet 2440mm × 1220mm
chipboard.

Battens

Cut from 25mm × 50mm PAR
4 ×	1082mm	A,B,G,H
5 ×	455mm	C,D,E,J,K
4 ×	400mm	L,M
2 ×	300mm	N,P

9m to allow a little for waste.
4 50mm hinges.
50 25mm no. 8 panhead
screws.
1 840mm × 600mm sheet
tracing paper.
6 A4 sheets carbon paper.

Children are not really keen on putting things in cupboards at the best of times, but the cheerful smiling porker on each door of this cupboard is the best possible encouragement for them to open the doors and put a few things away.

Chipboard is perfectly adequate for many of the projects in this book but the ears on the doors and the trotters that form the legs of this cupboard are not supported, so they will probably break off if they are not made out of plywood. Fortunately there is no reason why the base and the back of the cupboard should not be made out of chipboard, so only one sheet of plywood is needed and so the cost stays within reasonable bounds.

It goes without saying that the way the intricate cutting-out on the front panel is done is the thing that will make or break this project. Provided that this is done carefully and the saw cut goes down vertically through the sheet, the door will fit well and the gap around the head will be only a couple of millimetres. But if you try and make the

doors from a separate piece of plywood, you will never be able to get such a close fit.

So a power jig saw is almost essential for this project. If you have a lot of patience, you might be able to do the job by hand with an ordinary coping saw but a pad saw is unlikely to be satisfactory because the blade will tend to wander off the vertical and go blunt quite quickly.

The basic plan provided here does not have a central partition, just a shelf. But there is no reason why you cannot fit one by the addition of two battens at top and bottom to slide the partition into, plus another batten each side of the partition to support the shelf, cut into two parts in this case. This variation would be very suitable if you intend to let two children share the storage space or it is intended for something like clothing.

Again, this cupboard was designed to rest on the floor but there is no reason why it cannot be wall-mounted. That would keep the floor clear and make it easier to clean and tidy the room.

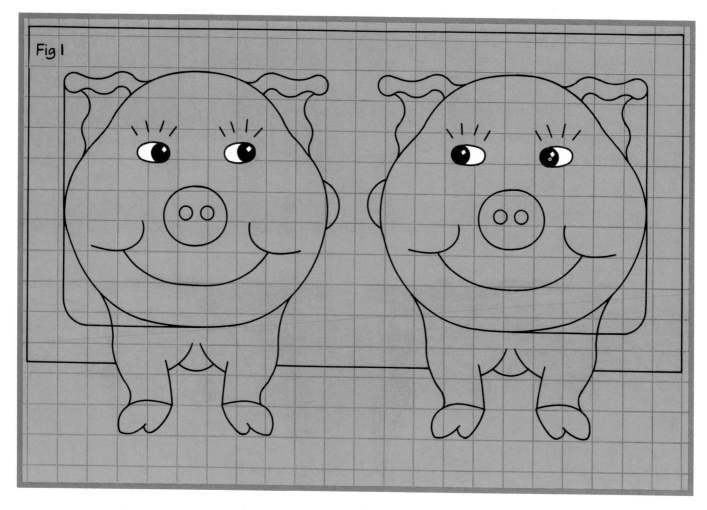

Fig 1

Marking Out

At first sight, the prospect of transfering a relatively complicated series of shapes from the page to a sheet of plywood may seem a daunting one. In practice, if you follow a few simple rules, it is not so difficult.

Begin by marking and cutting out two rectangles of plywood, one 1100mm × 660mm and the other 1100mm × 720mm.

Draw a line on the inside (rougher) face of all four panels 115mm up from the bottom of one of the longer sides. On the inside of

the 660mm high panel (which will be the front panel), draw another line 175mm up from the bottom and a vertical line 60mm in from either side. These last two lines will give you the bottom and the outer edges of the doors.

Now, mark out your tracing paper in a grid of 50mm squares. This is your basic grid for drawing one half of one pig and corresponds to the larger squares in Fig. 1. You can now sketch in the right-hand half of the pig's face, tummy and one leg, omitting the eyeballs for the time being.

The left-hand edge of your tracing paper is the centreline of the pig.

When you are happy with your artistry, lay your carbon paper on the inside of the front panel, covering the right-hand third of the panel but not overlapping the lines showing the position of the bottom and side of the door. Make sure the carbon side faces down. Now lay your tracing paper on top of the carbon paper in such a way that the pig's

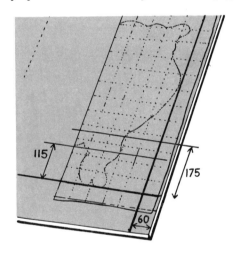

chin is resting on the line that indicates the bottom of the door and its cheek and ear are on the line that indicates the side of the door. Trace out the right-hand side of the head and the leg and mark the vertical centreline on the chin and the top of the head. You do not need to trace in any of the features at this stage. Now move the carbon paper until it covers the area where the left-hand side of the pig's head will be, turn the tracing paper over and line up the centreline on the top of the head and on the chin. Trace out your lines, then repeat the operations for the other head and legs. Finally,

mark out the finger holes around part of the base of an aerosol can or something with a diameter of about 65mm and mark the rounded corners at the bottom of the doors.

Cutting Out

Drill a hole in each finger grip and start cutting out the doors from there. Then cut out the outside of the front panel where necessary.

Once this panel has been cut out, you can use it as a pattern for marking the trotters on the rear panel. The bottom of the cupboard will then be on the line you drew 115mm up from the bottom of the panel. Draw another line across the top of the rear panel 670mm up from the lower line (50mm down from the top of the panel). You can now draw in the two rumps with a smooth and regular curve between the upper line and the top of the panel. Make sure that the outline is identical on both sides. If you stand both panels up on their legs, the upper line on the rear panel should be 10mm above the top of the front panel. If it is not, re-check your measurements.

When you are satisfied with the outline, cut out the rear panel as

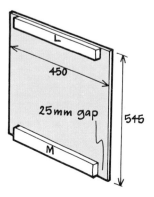

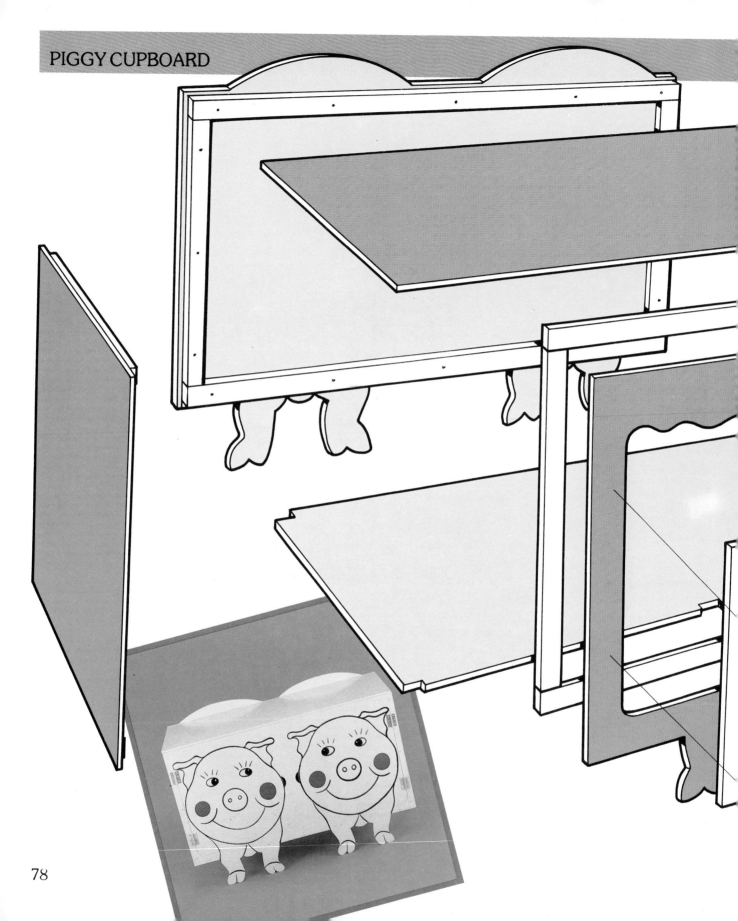

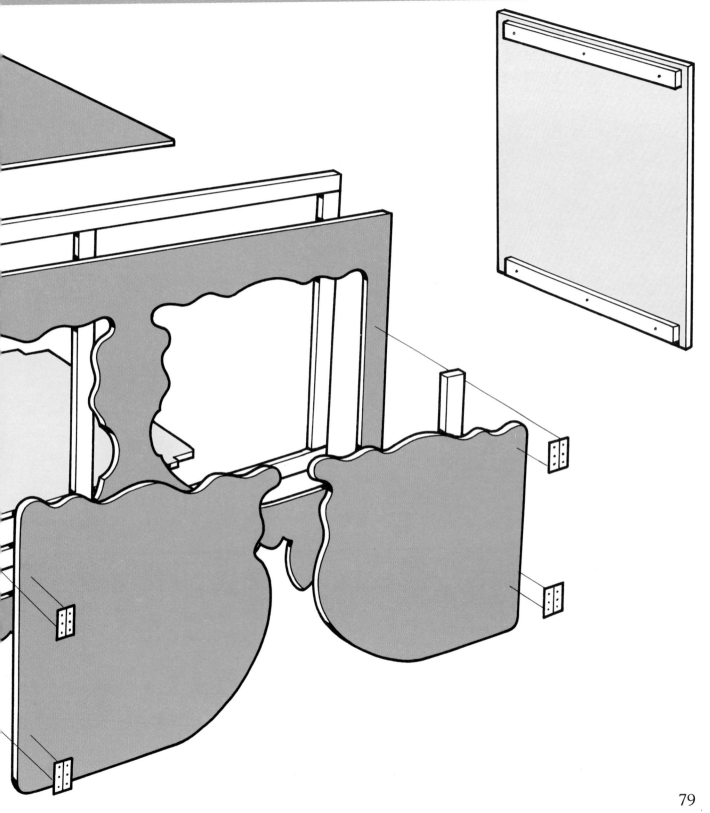

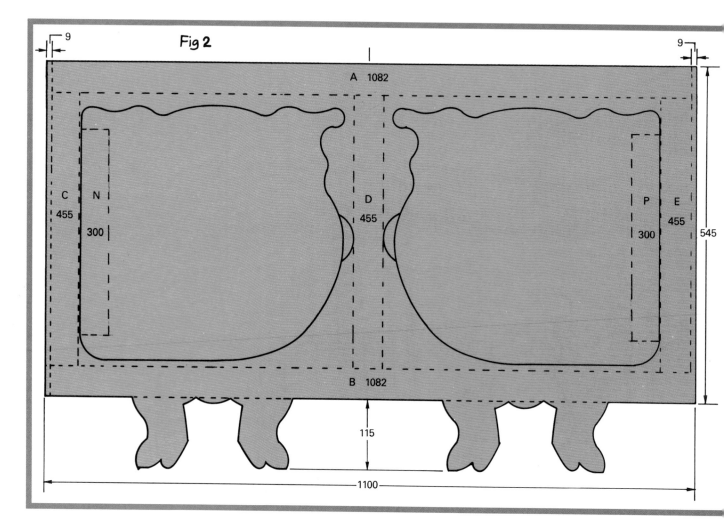

Fig 2

9

A 1082

C 455

N

300

D 455

P 300

E 455

545

9

B 1082

115

1100

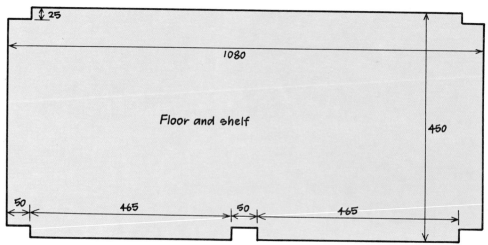

25

1080

Floor and shelf

450

50   465   50   465

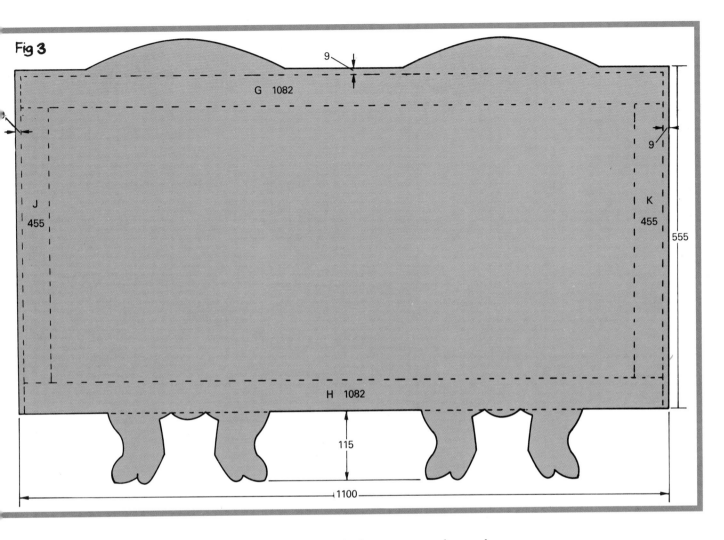

Fig 3

shown in Fig.3 and check it against the front panel again. Measure and cut out the top panel, the two side panels plus the floor and the shelf at this point.

Battens

Cut the battens to the lengths shown at the beginning of this section. Sand and slightly bevel the edges. Drill a series of 4mm diameter holes through the 50mm face of each batten, one hole 50mm or so in from either end and the others at 300mm – 450mm intervals, making sure that there are at least three holes in each batten and five in the long ones. In the case of the battens N and P on the inside of the doors, the screw holes must be drilled 25mm in from either end.

Take one batten and one panel at a time and apply adhesive to the 50mm face of the batten which will be in contact with the panel.

Locate batten A on the inside, rougher face of the front panel in such a way that its top edge is flush with the top edge of the panel and so that there is a gap of 9mm at either end between the ends of the batten and the edges of the panel. Screw down. Fix batten B in a similar manner flush with the bottom edge of the panel.

Fix batten C with its outer edge 9mm in from the outside of the panel and between battens A and B. There will be a gap between the ends of batten C and the edges of battens A and B. This is because the battens have been planed to less than their original 25mm × 50mm in the finishing process. This does not matter. Repeat this operation for batten E, then fix batten D exactly in the middle of the panel, as shown in Fig.2.

Fix battens N and P to the inside face of the doors. Turn the front panel over so that the battens are underneath. Place the doors in position, making sure that there is a more or less equal gap all the way round. Place the hinges approximately in position and mark the centres of the screw holes. Make a starter hole with a nail or bradawl

and drill with a 2mm diameter bit to a depth of about 12mm. Screw on both of the hinges now.

On the inside face of the rear panel, mark a point at either side 660mm up from the bottom of the panel (10mm down from the bottom of the rump).

Fix batten G 9mm in from either side of the panel and with its top edge on the two marks you have just made. If you stand both front and back panels on their legs, the top edge of batten G should be level with the top of the front panel.

Fix batten H 9mm in from either edge of the panel and with its bottom edge flush with the bottom edge of the panel. Fix battens J and K with their outer edges 9mm in from the edges of the panel between batten G and H.

Fix battens L and M to the inside faces of the two side panels in such a way that they are flush with the top and bottom of the panel respec-

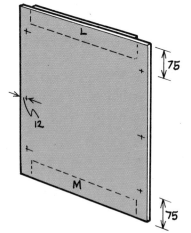

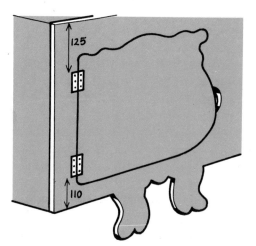

tively and with a gap of 25mm at either end. Drill three 4mm diameter holes 12mm in from the vertical edges of the side panels.

Assembly

Hold the front panel upright and position one of the side panels (battens on the inside) against batten C in such a way that it is level with the front panel at top and bottom. Screw through the side panel into batten C, making sure that there is no gap between the edge of the side panel and the inside face of the front panel. Raise the rear panel into position and screw through into batten J, making sure the side panel is lined up at the bottom with bottom of the rear panel and at the top with the top edge of batten G.

Drill a series of 4mm diameter holes 12mm in from the edges of the floor panel at about 400mm intervals. Pull the open end of the assembly apart slightly and slide the floor into position until it is resting on battens B, H and M. You can now screw the other side into position, lining up as before.

Make sure that the front and rear panels of the cupboard are pulled well together, so that there is no gap between the edge of the floor and the inside faces of the panels, and screw down the floor into battens B, H and M.

If you intend to screw the cupboard to a wall or fill it with heavy items, it is best to glue as well as screw all the panels together. This will make the pig very rigid and so it will stand up to the strain better.

Drill a series of 4mm diameter holes in the top panel as shown below. Place it in position with its front and side edges flush with the front and side panels and screw down into battens A, G and L.

If you feel that your kids are likely to put extra strain on the cupboard, or if it has to sit on an uneven floor, consider joining each pair of trotters with a short length of batten. Trim the battens so that they do not stick out at all, pin and glue them into place on the 25mm edge and paint them all an inconspicuous colour.

Painting

The carpentry for this unit is now complete. All that remains is to paint it, following the guidelines set out in the introduction. Once the background painting has been done, you can transfer the features to the front panel using your tracing paper and carbon paper as before. Add the eyeballs at this stage, then paint in the features, allowing one colour to dry well before painting in an adjoining colour.

The piggy shown in these pages is painted white, but there is no reason why the doors cannot be painted an authentic piggy pink to contrast with the rest of the cupboard. Where the cupboard is screwed to the wall or it fits into one definite position in the room, you could paint a pink curly tail on the wall to complete the picture in every detail except for the squeak.

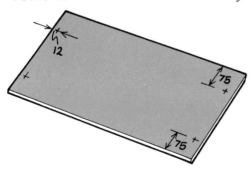

Bulldog Sofa

This Bulldog does not snap unless there are too many people sitting on his back.

Like the Piggy cupboard, the Bulldog sofa is bound to get harder wear than the beds and the desks described in this book, so there is no real alternative to plywood for its construction. But as only one sheet of material is required, this project remains at a competitive price compared with anything in the shops and it can even be left outside in the garden for the odd night without becoming too bedraggled.

The most testing part of this project is cutting out the main end pieces in the shape of the bulldog, though this is less critical than cutting out the doors and the front panel of the Piggy cupboard because there is no need to get two pieces to fit accurately in this case.

Cutting the Panels

The first part of the job consists of cutting two smaller panels out of your sheet of plywood, each 600mm × 830mm. Then you transfer the outline of the bulldog on to these panels by means of the tracing paper and carbon paper. This may sound rather complicated to start with but provided that you follow the instructions carefully, it comes out quite easily in the end.

If the sofa is going to stand in a corner, the end with the tail must stand next to the wall and you must mark out the end pieces in such a way that the tail is positioned behind the sitter rather than in front. All that you have to do is select the smooth face of the sheet, arrange it so that it is next to the sitter and lay the tracing paper down on to the sheet the appropriate way round. It is best to keep the smooth face on the inside of this unit, next to the sitter, because that will help to prevent anybody getting splinters.

Marking Out

With the 600mm side of the tracing paper towards you draw a vertical line down the middle of the sheet. This will be your centre-line. Now draw six vertical lines, 50mm apart to the right of the centre line, and a series of horizontal lines all the way up the right hand half of the page, starting 10mm up from the bottom. This forms the grid for marking out. Each of the 50mm squares on your panel represents one large square in Figs.1 and 2. You can now start sketching in the shape of both ends on the same piece of tracing paper. Do not draw in the features at this stage.

When you are satisfied with your

Materials
1 sheet 2440mm × 1220mm 9mm plywood.

Battens
Cut from 25mm × 50mm PAR

2	× 400mm	A
2	× 200mm	B
1	× 900mm	C
1	× 850mm	D

Say 3.5m to allow for off-cuts.
1 600mm × 840mm sheet tracing paper.
6 A4 sheets carbon paper.

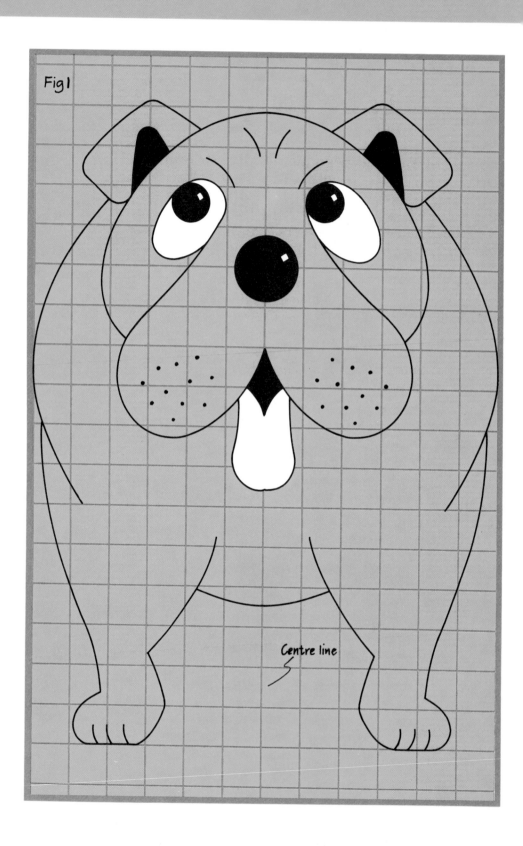

Fig 1

Centre line

draughtsmanship, mark the centre-line on one of your 600mm × 830mm panels. Remember to do your marking out on the smoother inside face of the panel. Cover the right hand side of the panel with carbon paper (carbon face down) so that it almost touches the cen-treline, the bottom edge and the right hand edge of the panel.

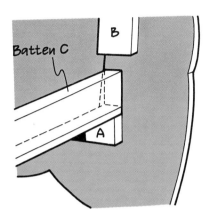

Now lay your tracing paper on the carbon paper, lining up your centre lines and with the bottom of the dog's paw flush with the bottom of the panel. Trace the shape on to the plywood checking that the out-line is being transferred. Do not trace the features at this stage.

Then lay the carbon paper (car-bon face down) on the left hand side of the panel, turn your tracing paper over and trace in the shape for the other side. Also on the inside face, mark out the position of the battens as shown in Fig.3 and below right. If you don't do it now, you will find it impossible to locate the points precisely once the shape has been cut out of the sheet.

Position batten A by drawing a line 350mm up from the bottom of the panel and then draw another, line X, 9mm above that one.

Then, mark a point 100mm in from the back edge of the panel and 680mm up from the base. This is point Z. Position the end of batten C so that it is sitting on line X with its back edge 200mm back from the centre line. Draw round the cross section of batten C. Point Y is now the top front corner of this batten. Connect points Y and Z and mark point V, 65mm up the line YZ from

line X, which will give you the posi-tion of the bottom end of batten B.

Mark the centreline on the other 600mm × 830mm panel (inside face). Using the shape you have just cut out as a pattern, mark out those parts of the shape which are com-mon to both ends. Then with the help of your carbon paper, as before, transfer the details of the hind legs and the tail from the trac-ing paper on to the chipboard.

Repeat the procedure for estab-lishing the position of the battens on the inside face of the other end panel. The positions of points V, Y and Z will appear the other way round. You can also cut out the shape of the other end panel and the other three panels that form the seat as shown over the page.

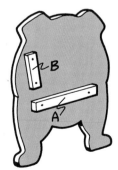

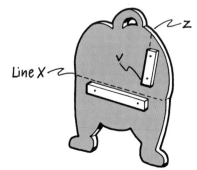

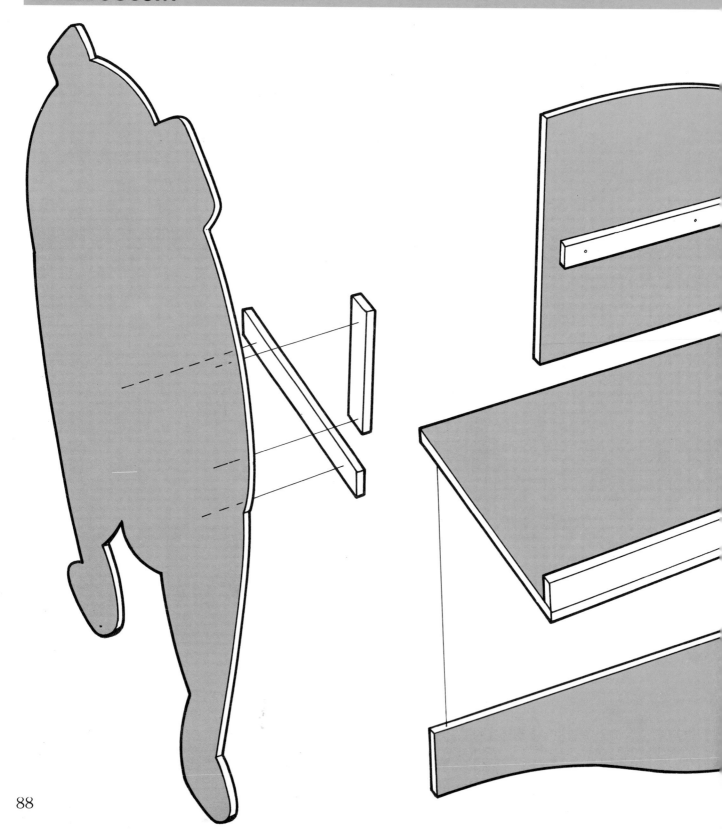

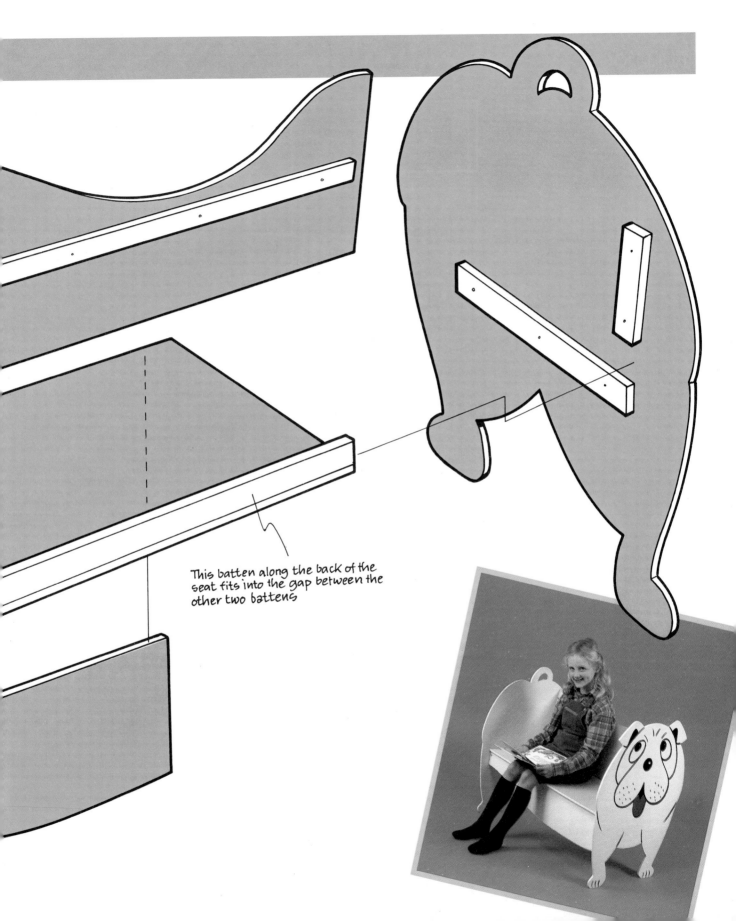

This batten along the back of the seat fits into the gap between the other two battens

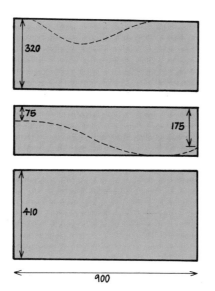

Locate batten C on the top side of the seat panel flush with the panel's back edge and sides. Now turn the panel over and screw through the panel into batten C.

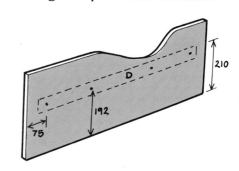

Drill a series of 4mm diameter holes 192mm up from the bottom of the seat back . Apply adhesive to one of the 50mm faces of batten D and locate it on the rear of the panel, with its top edge 210mm up from the bottom of the panel and a 25mm gap either end. Screw through the panel into batten D.

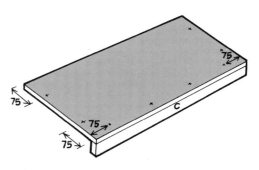

Finally, drill two 4mm diameter holes 12mm in from each edge of the seat panel and 50mm from the back and the front so that you can screw it down at the sides.

Battens

Cut the battens to the lengths shown at the beginning of this section. Sand and bevel the edges and corners as necessary. Drill two 4mm diameter holes in each batten A and B 25mm in from each end. Apply adhesive to the 50mm face of the batten that will be in contact with the panel and work on one panel and one batten at a time.

Locate batten A on the inside face of the panel so that its top edge is on the line already drawn 350mm up from the bottom of the panel and so that its ends are 200mm either side of the centreline. Screw down evenly all the way along. Fix batten (B) to the inside face of the panel so that its front edge is on the line ZY and with its bottom end at point V. Repeat these operations on the inside face of the other end.

Drill a series of 4mm diameter holes 12mm in from the back edge of the seat panel. Apply adhesive to one of the 25mm faces of batten C.

Assembly

For the start of the assembly process, you will need the help of an extra pair of hands. Ask your helper

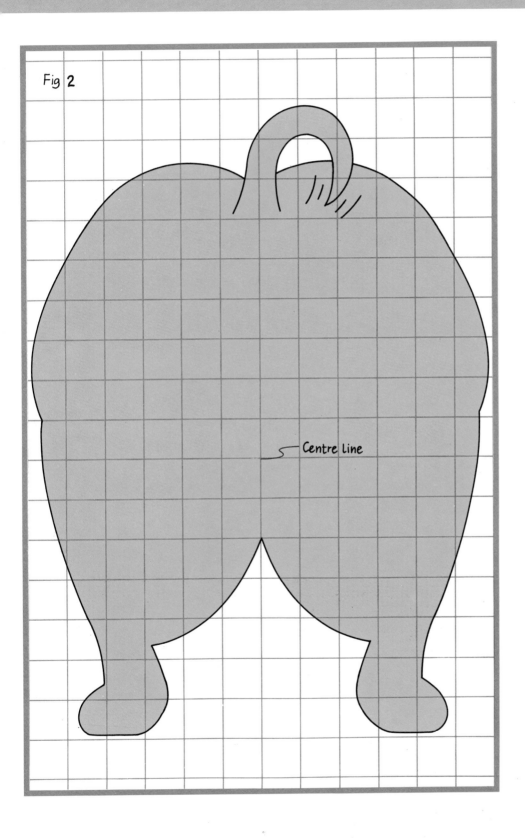

Fig 2

Centre line

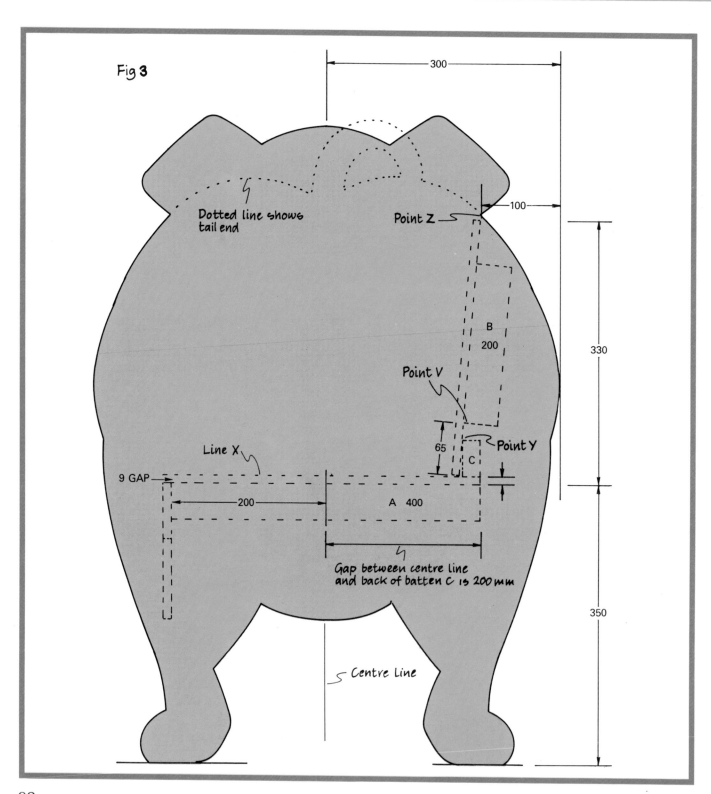

Fig 3

300

Dotted line shows tail end

Point Z

100

B
200

330

Point V

65

Point Y

Line X

C

9 GAP

200

A 400

350

Gap between centre line
and back of batten C is 200 mm

Centre Line

to hold the end panels upright while you place the seat panel in position with batten C on top once more and at the back. The rear edge should be flush with the rear end of battens A and there should be no gap between the sides of the panel and inside faces of the end panels. The front edge will overhang the front of battens A by 10mm. Screw through the seat into battens A. Glue the panels into place if you want to make a really good job. The seat should now stand up on its own.

Drill two 4mm diameter holes 12mm in from either edge of the

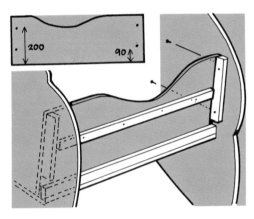

rear panel. Position this panel with the batten at the back so that it is touching batten C at the bottom and resting against battens B. Make sure there is no gap between the edges of the rear panel and the inside faces of the end panels. Screw the panel to battens B.

Drill a 4mm diameter hole 25mm down from the top of the front panel and 12mm in from either end. Then position the front panel so that its top edge is tight underneath the overhanging seat panel. Make sure there is no gap at the ends between

the edges of the front panel and the inside faces of the end panels. Screw through the front panel into the ends of battens A.

Painting

You have now completed the construction stage of this project. Everything depends on painting it carefully so that it resists the rain and the attention of the children for as long as possible.

Before you apply the finishing coats, you could try painting the entire sofa with either a polyurethane varnish or a mixture of PVA wood glue and water in the ratio of 3 parts water to one part of PVA adhesive. This will seal the surface of the plywood and also tend to hold the surface together so that there are no splinters. Then paint the whole unit with undercoat, leaving out the primer stage as that is not necessary once you have sealed the surface with varnish or PVA.

Next, paint the whole thing with the basic finishing colour. In the photographs this is white but it could be buff or even an outrageous colour like pink. When the base colour is thoroughly dry – allow at least 36 hours – mark on the features using the carbon paper and tracing paper method described earlier. Pay particular attention when you paint the tongue as the red paint could run into the black paint if you are not careful. The design of the eyeballs and the whiskers is particularly important because that gives the expression to the face. Copy the design given in Fig.1 exactly.

Elephant Slide and Playhouse

This pachyderm packs in a Slide and a Playhouse, so your kids will never forget the fun they had with the Elephant.

Materials
4 sheets 2440mm × 1220mm exterior grade 9mm plywood.

Battens
Cut from 25mm × 50mm PAR
2 × 1700mm   A
2 ×   625mm   B
2 ×   950mm   C
2 ×   550mm   D,E
5 ×   700mm   F,G,H,J,K
12m of 25mm × 50mm batten, allowing a little for waste.
2 or 3   75mm hinges (aluminium or galvanised).
2 magnetic door catches.

As set out in the plan, the Elephant slide and Playhouse is strictly for outside use due to its size. It follows that the Elephant must be made out of exterior grade plywood so that it resists the weather and is strong enough for the boisterous kind of play that it is designed for.

The Elephant is identical on both sides except for the door, so you have to decide on the number and the position of the doors before you start marking out. You must use the smoothest piece of plywood that you have available with the good side facing upwards and outward for the surface of the slide because the consequences of splinters are quite unthinkable!

Marking Out
Start with two of the plywood sheets and mark one of them out in 150mm × 150mm squares starting from the bottom right hand side of the sheet so as to form the grid for the design. Take the shape indicated on the plan and transfer it to the sheet square by square, bearing in mind that each 150mm square on

the plywood is represented by one large square on the plan. Do not bother marking in the details of the tusks, eye or ears at this stage. On the other hand, you must mark the positions for the battens before cutting out the shape because these are all given from the edge of the plywood sheet.

Draw a line 1000mm up from the bottom of the panel (200mm down from the top) starting at a point W 300mm in from the back edge and continuing to a point X 925mm in from the back edge. This will give you the position of the top edge of batten B. Mark a point Y 75mm up from the bottom edge of the panel and 75mm in from the front edge of the panel. Then draw a line between X and Y. This will give you the position of the top of batten A.

Mark a point Z on the bottom edge of the panel 150mm in from the rear edge. Draw a line between Z and W – this will give you the position of the rear edge of batten C. Cut out this side panel, including the door if there is one.

On the inside face of the other

94

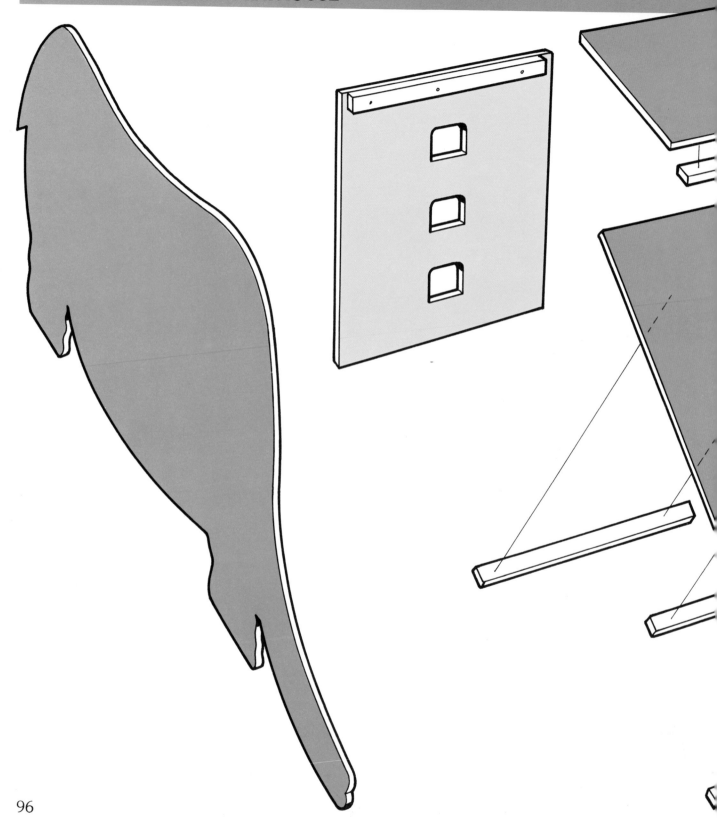

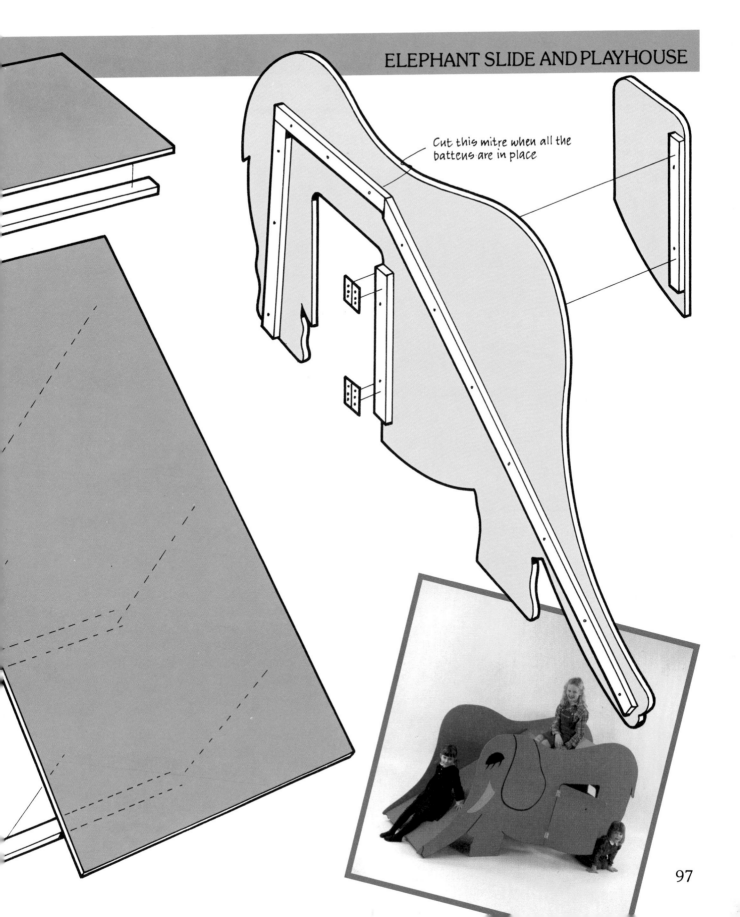

Cut this mitre when all the battens are in place

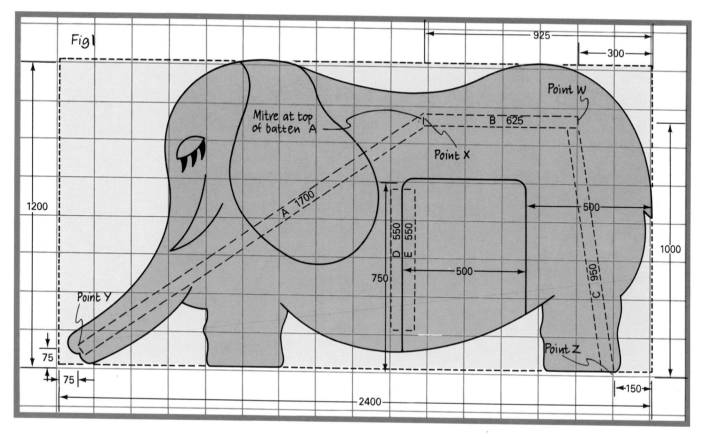

Fig 1

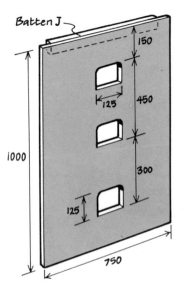

Batten J

2440mm × 1220mm panel, mark out the position of the battens as before remembering that this side panel will face the other way round! Then using the first side as a pattern, mark the shape on the other sheet (otherway round) and cut it out, including the door if there is to be one. Mark and cut out the slide panel, the top panel, and the rear panel.

Battens

Cut the battens to the lengths shown at the beginning of this section. Sand and bevel the edges and corners as necessary. Take one side panel at a time and lay the battens on the lines you have drawn. Mark

and cut the mitre at the top end of batten A.

Drill a series of 4mm diameter holes through the 50mm face of all battens, except batten K, one hole 50mm in from either end, and the others at 300mm or so intervals. Screw and glue the battens in position as shown in Fig.1. Repeat this procedure on the inside face of the other side panel.

Drill 3 holes through the 50mm face of batten D and batten E, one 25mm from either end and one in the middle. Screw and glue these battens into position either side of the front edge of the doorway as shown on the next page. Turn the panel over and locate the hinges.

Put a couple of off-cuts under the door so that it is level with the side panel. Position the door so that there is an even gap all round and mark the screw holes. Make a starter hole with a bradawl, then drill 2mm diameter holes to a depth of 12mm. Screw hinges into position.

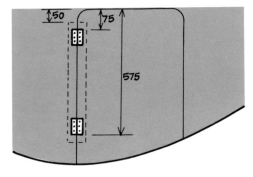

Glue and screw the battens F, G and H to the underside of the slide panel as shown on the right. There should be a gap of 25mm between the ends of the battens and the edge of the panel. Fix batten J to the inside of the rear panel, in such a way that its top edge is flush with the top of the panel and with a 25mm gap at either end.

Drill a row of 4mm diameter holes through the top panel 62mm back from the front (750mm) edge. Apply adhesive to one of the 25mm faces of batten K and locate it on the underside of the top panel, with its front edge 50mm back from the edge of the panel and with a 25mm gap at either end. Screw through the top panel into batten K.

Assembly
Drill a row of 4mm diameter holes 12mm in from the edges of the slide, the top and the rear panels so you can screw the elephant together.

For the assembly process, at least for the early stages, you are going to need an assistant to hold the panels in position for you while you screw them together. Ask your assistant to hold both of the side panels upright, battens on the inside, while you position the top panel overlapping the rear end of batten B at the back by 11mm. Make sure that the top panel is tight up against the inside face of the side panel and then screw down through the holes already drilled in the panel into battens B at each side. Glue the panel in place if you want to build in the maximum strength.

Position the rear panel, batten on the inside, tightly between the two sides and tight underneath the overhanging top panel. Screw through the rear panel into battens C. Position the slide panel tightly between the two side panels and tight underneath the overhang of the top panel. Screw through the slide panel into battens A. Fit the door catch.

Painting
The Elephant is now fully assembled and ready for painting inside and out. Do not be tempted to leave the inside of the Playhouse unpainted because even exterior grade plywood does get attacked by moisture in the air over a period of time. When the finishing coat has dried for a couple of days, mark the tusks, the eyes and the ears on the sides and paint them in carefully. If the slide is not 'fast' enough, polish it with car polish.

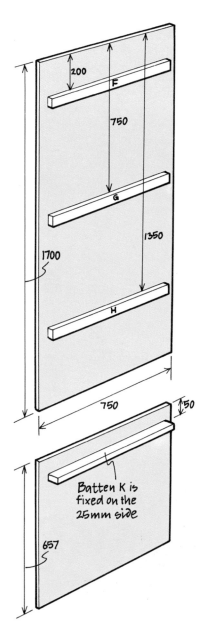

Batten K is fixed on the 25mm side

Hippo Slide and Playhouse

This happy Hippo almost blushes with pleasure when the kids whizz down the Slide built over the top of the Playhouse.

The Hippo slide is similar in design and concept to the Elephant slide but is rather more difficult to make because the outline of the side is a little more complicated. As with the Elephant, the most important thing to check is the smoothness of the various sheets of plywood that you have bought. Mark the smooth sides with a pencil and cut the panel for the slide out of the best piece of plywood you have. Arrange the smooth side facing outwards to provide the optimum slide surface. As for all the other panels, arrange the smooth side outwards so that the exterior of the Playhouse is as well finished as possible.

Marking Out

You will first need to decide which way round you want the Hippo to face and in which side you want the door, though there is nothing to stop you having a door in both sides if you want to.

Take two sheets of plywood and on the rougher face of one of these sheets, mark out 150mm × 150mm squares starting from the bottom left corner. Transfer the design for the shape to be cut out square by square (1 square drawn on the plywood = 1 square on the plan). Do not mark in the face at this stage.

You will need to mark out the position of the battens first, as shown on Fig.1, before cutting out the shape since the dimensions are given from the edge of the complete sheet. So draw a line 1000mm up from the bottom of the panel (200mm down from the top) starting at point W 300mm in from the back edge and continuing to point X 925mm in from the back edge. This will give you the position of the top edge of batten B.

Mark point Y 125mm up from the bottom edge of the panel and 150mm in from the front edge of the panel. Then draw a line between X and Y. This will give you the position of the top of batten A. Mark point Z on the bottom edge of the panel 300mm in from the rear edge. Draw a line between Z and W — this will give you the position of the rear edge of batten C. Cut out this side panel, including door if there is one.

Materials

4 sheets 2440mm × 1220mm exterior grade 9mm plywood.

Battens

Cut from 25mm × 50mm PAR

2 ×	1625mm	A
2 ×	625mm	B
2 ×	950mm	C
2 ×	600mm	D,E
5 ×	700mm	F,G,H,J,K

Say 12m to allow for off-cuts.
2 or 3 75mm hinges (aluminium or galvanised).
2 magnetic door catches.

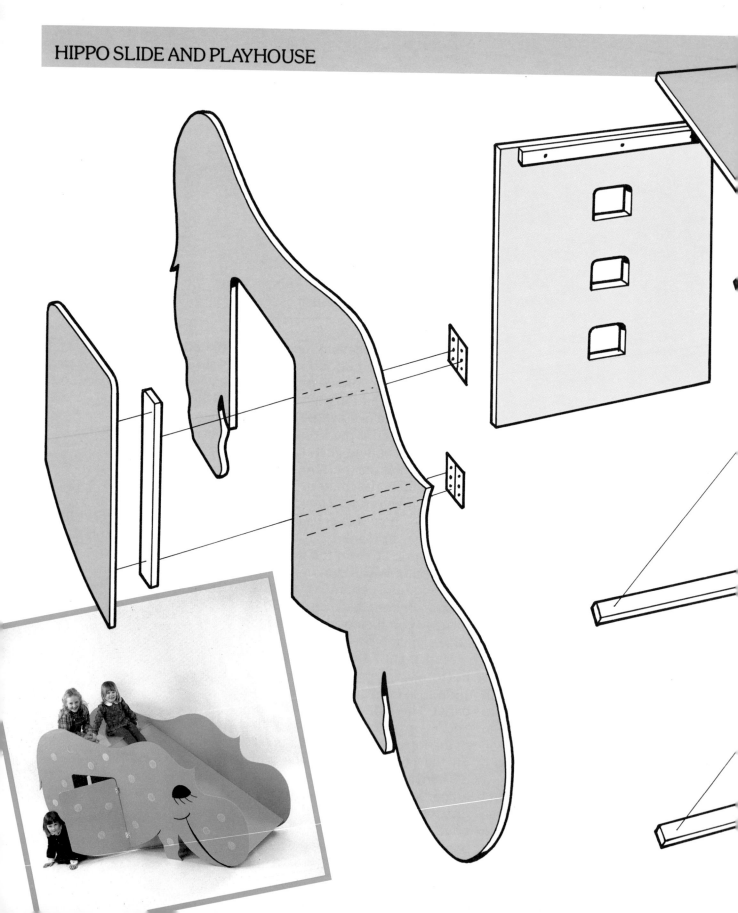

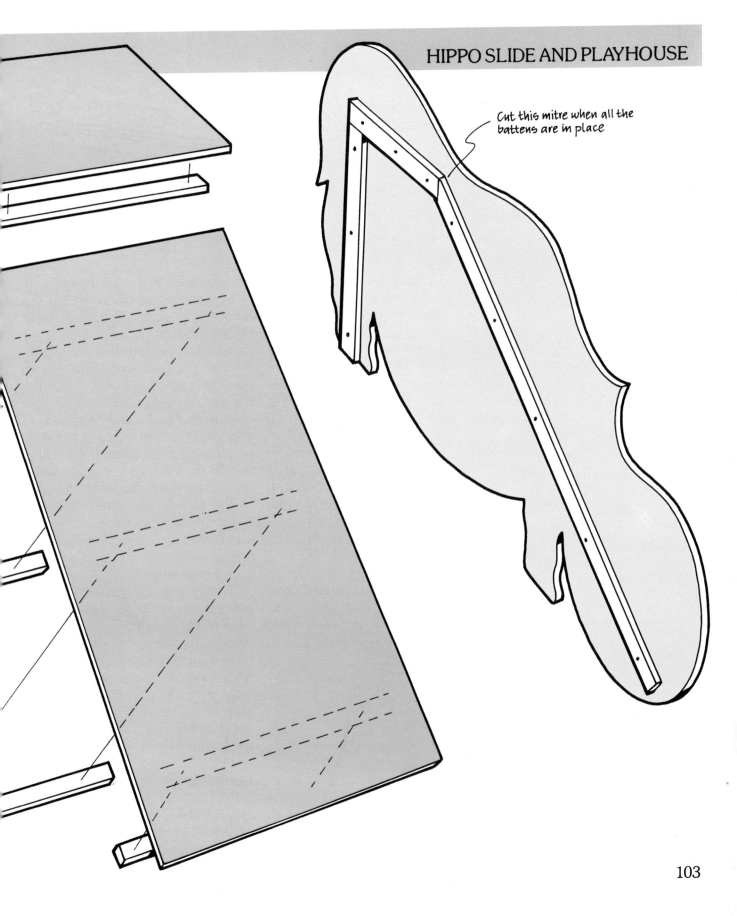

Cut this mitre when all the battens are in place

On the inside face of the other panel, mark out the position of the battens in reverse. Then using the first side as a pattern, mark the outline on the other side and cut out. Mark and cut out the slide panel, the top panel, and the rear panel as well.

Battens

Cut the battens to the lengths shown at the beginning of this section. Sand and bevel the edges and corners. Take one side panel at a time and lay the battens exactly in place on the lines you have drawn. You can then mark and cut the mitre at the top end of batten A from the other battens without the need for any further measurement.

Drill a series of 4mm diameter holes through the 50mm face of all battens, except for battens D, E and K, one hole 50mm in from either end and the others at 300mm or so intervals. Screw and glue the battens in position as shown in Fig.1.

Drill 3 holes through the 50mm face of batten D and batten E, one 25mm from either end and one in the middle. Screw and glue these battens into position either side of

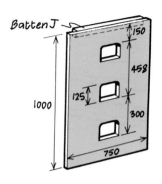

the front edge of the doorway.

Turn the panel over and lay the hinges in position. Put a couple of batten off-cuts under the door, so that it sits level with the side panel. Position the door so that there is an even gap all round and screw the hinges into place.

Glue and screw the battens F, G and H to the underside of the slide panel as shown on the right. There should be a gap of 25mm between the ends of the battens and the edge of the panel. Fix batten J to the inside of the rear panel, in such a way that its top edge is flush with the top of the panel and with a 25mm gap at either end.

Drill a row of 4mm diameter holes through the top panel 62mm back from the front (750mm) edge. Apply adhesive to one of the 25mm faces of batten K and locate it on the underside of the top panel, with its front edge 50mm back from the edge of the panel and with a 25mm gap at either end. Screw through the top panel into batten K.

Assembly

Drill a row of 4mm diameter holes, about 250mm apart, 12mm in from the edges of the slide and the top and rear panels so you can screw

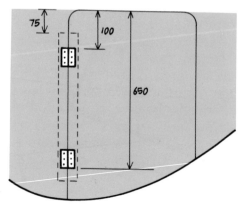

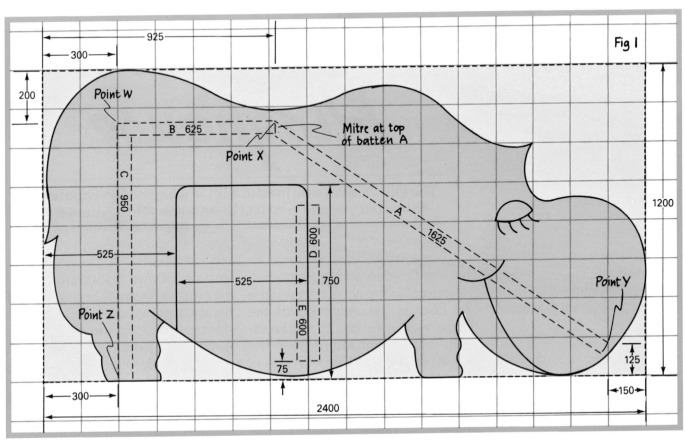

Fig I

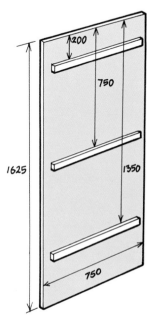

the whole thing together. You will now need some assistance for the early stages of assembly.

Ask your helper to hold both side panels upright while you drop the top panel into position. The rear edge of the panel should overlap the rear end of batten B at the back by 11mm. Make sure the top panel is tight up against the inside face of the side panel and screw down through it into battens B. You can glue all these panels into place as well as screw them, if you want to make a really strong unit.

Position the rear panel, battens on the inside, tightly between the two sides and tight underneath the overhanging top panel. Screw through the rear panel into battens C. Position the slide panel, battens underneath, tightly between the two side panels and tight underneath the overhang of the top panel. Screw through the slide panel into battens A.

Painting

All that remains now is to paint the Hippo starting inside. As this is such an amiable beast it is important to capture the happy expression on the animal's face, so allow plenty of time for this final stage of the work and follow the method laid down for the Elephant slide.

Old Boot Playhouse

The Old Woman who lived in a Shoe whipped her children to bed but you can just send them out to the Playhouse.

Materials

5 sheets 2440mm × 1220mm exterior grade 9mm plywood.

Battens

Cut from 25mm × 50mm PAR

2 ×	1200mm	A
2 ×	600mm	B
2 ×	175mm	C
2 ×	950mm	D
2 ×	1275mm	E
4 ×	550mm	F,G,M,N
3 ×	1150mm	P,Q,V

Say 18m to allow for off-cuts.
Quadrant beading
Weatherstripping
3 hinges
1 door lock
Glazing material

This is the biggest and most impressive project in the book because the Old Boot is the only one of the playhouses with plenty of headroom for older children. Even the Old Woman would find plenty of room for her children in this shoe.

There is no question at all of building this project for use inside unless you bring it down to half scale. You could do this by working to a 75mm square instead of a 150mm square when you are doing the marking out. Then you would end up with a Playhouse one quarter the size of the one shown in the photographs though that would still be large for inside use.

Nevertheless, the best way of making this unit is in exterior plywood so that you can assemble it in the garden. Provided that you glaze the windows, put draught strips around the door and seal any gaps between the panels with mastic, the Old Boot can stay outside perfectly happily for three or four years.

Mark out the smooth side of one of the sheets of plywood into squares 150mm × 150mm. Start off measuring from the bottom left hand corner of the first sheet and transfer the outline of the Boot given in Fig.1 on to the sheet. Each square on the plan represents one of the 150mm squares on the sheet. Do not bother marking in the details at this stage.

Then mark point X at the top of the grid, 175mm in from the rear edge and point Y 1525mm in from the front edge of the grid. Also mark point V at the bottom of the panel 225mm in from the front edge.

Next, mark point W 225mm in from the front edge of the panel and 950mm up from the bottom of the panel (250mm down from the top of the grid) and point Z at the bottom 175mm in from the rear edge. Draw in the lines V-W and X-Z. Mark point T 184mm down from the top of the grid and 1575mm in from the front edge. Draw in the line W-T. Mark point S, 175mm down from the top of the grid and 1525mm back from the front of the panel. Draw in the line S-Y.

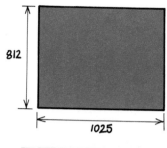

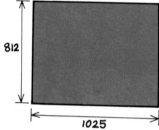

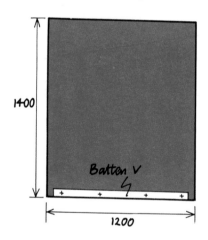

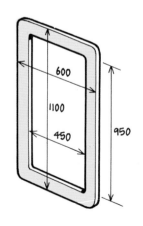

Cutting Out

When you have marked out one side complete, cut it out and then mark points X, Y and V plus the positions for the battens on the other sheet. Remember that these will appear to be in reverse for the second side. Next lay the first side on to the second side so that points V and Z line up accurately and then carefully trace the outline of the panel you have already cut out on to the marked sheet.

Cut out the second side and then mark and cut out the shapes of the two end panels and the gable that fits in the middle plus all three roof panels. You will be able to cut the two end panels from one sheet of plywood while the rest of the panels can be got out of the remaining sheet.

Glazed Version

Before you go any further, you must decide whether or not you want to build a glazed version of the Playhouse. If you do want to let the light in through proper windows, glass is ruled out for obvious reasons. The best materials for this purpose are Lexan which is almost bulletproof, or Perspex/Oroglass which are more or less identical and more or less shatterproof provided they are used in the 4mm thick variety.

You could also use Darvic which is again shatterproof but which transmits much less light than the materials mentioned already. Do not use the thinner and cheaper grades of transparent plastic for this job as it will be impossible to waterproof them and they could easily get blown in by the wind.

You need three pieces of plastic material for the glazing, one at 500mm × 500mm and two at 375mm × 425mm. Cut the front window aperture out to 450mm × 450mm and the side windows to 325mm × 375mm as shown in Figs. 3 and 4. Fix the glazing into place using closely spaced pop rivets or small machine screws. In either case, use large washers on both sides of the fixing to avoid the possibility of the rivet or the screw cutting into the surface of the plywood or the plastic.

Unglazed Version

If you are not going to bother glazing the Playhouse, you can either paint the windows in rather than cut them out, or you can simply leave them as open apertures. The edges of any open apertures should be finished very carefully as there is a strong possibility that the kids could pick up splinters from the cut edges of the plywood otherwise. Remember to cover up the apertures over the winter or you might find that the damp has allowed mildew to get a hold on the plywood despite the paint.

Fitting the Door

Mark out the door on the rear panel as shown in Fig. 3 and then cut it out with the corners rounded off to avoid splinters. Use the opening to mark out an inner door frame, overlapping the aperture by half an inch all round. The frame should be about three inches wide overall. You may have enough plywood to make

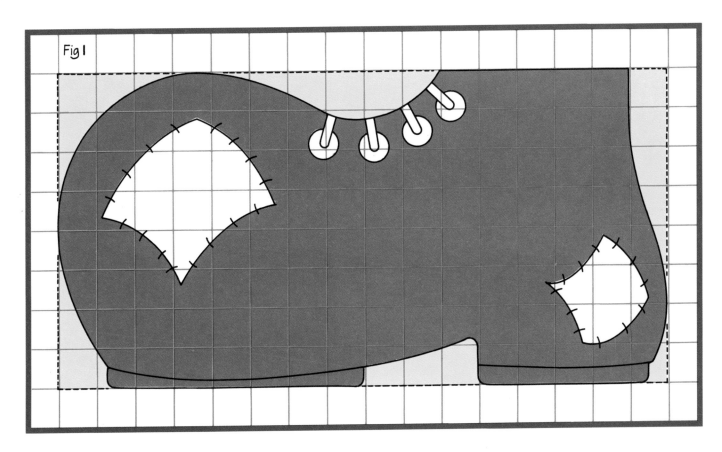

Fig I

this frame in one piece but if you have to make it from off-cuts it does not matter at all.

Pin and glue the frame around the door and then fix the door in place with three hinges as shown here. Be careful when you are fixing the hinges to the door as you only have the 9mm thickness of the plywood to screw into – remember to use screws that do not stick through the other side of the wood.

As the Old Boot will be outside in all weathers, fit a good door catch or lock to the door to prevent it being blown about in the wind. Fit strips of draught excluder around the inner frame to keep leaves and dust out as far as possible in bad weather.

Battens

Cut the battens to the lengths shown at the beginning of this section. Sand and bevel the edges and corners as necessary.

Drill a series of 4mm diameter holes centrally through the 50mm face of all the battens, except batten Y, one hole 50mm in from either end of battens A, B, C, D, E, F, G, M, N, P and Q and the others spaced evenly at 300mm or less intervals so that every batten has at least three holes in it. Take one batten and one panel at a time, starting with one of the side panels.

Screw and glue batten A in position with its rear edge on line X-Z so that the ends are flush with the top

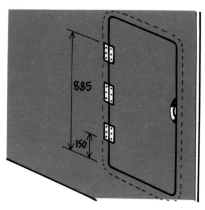

885

150

109

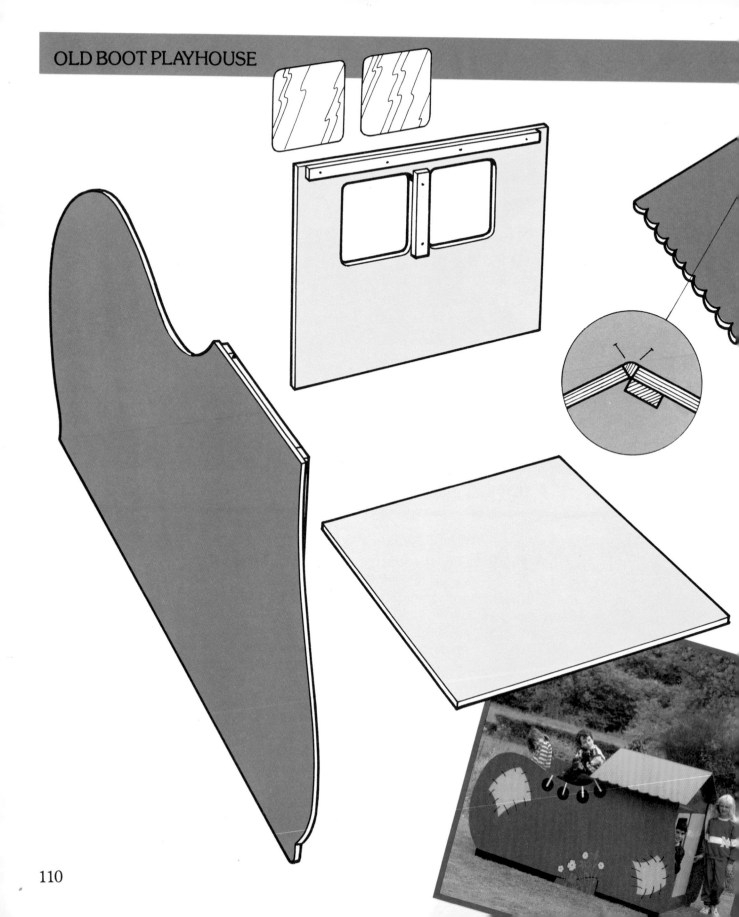

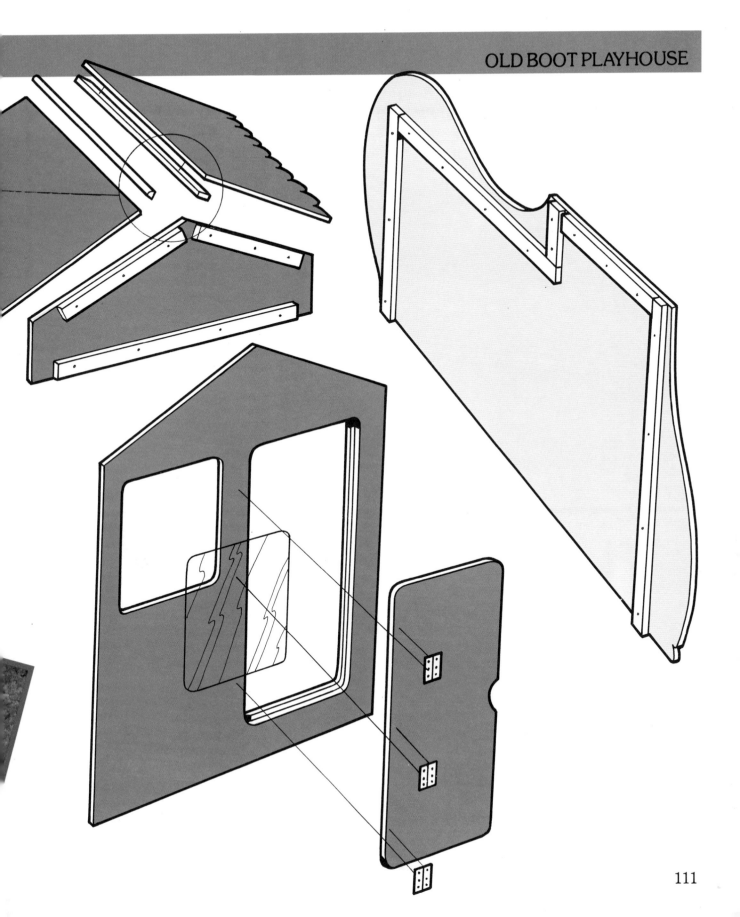

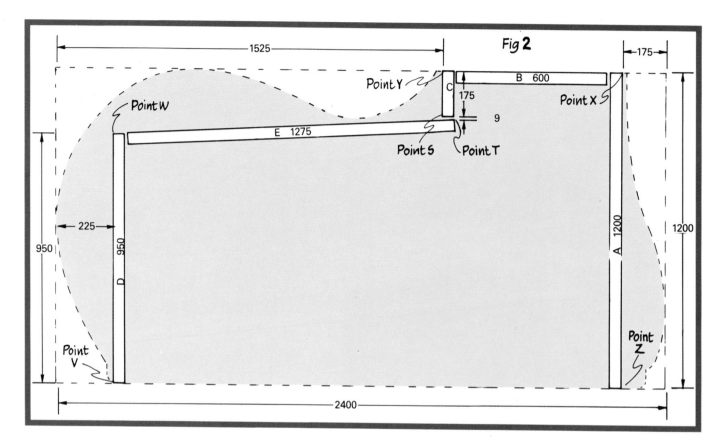

Fig 2

and bottom of the panel. Fix batten C with its front on line Y-S and its top end flush with the top of the panel. Fix batten B with its top edge flush with the top of the panel approximately midway between battens A and C. Fix batten D in position with its front edge on line V-W and its bottom end flush with the bottom edge of the panel. Fix batten E in position with its top edge on line W-T and in such a way that its rear top corner is on point T.

Fix battens F and G to the inside face of the rear panel so that their top edges are flush with the top edge of the panel and so that their top ends touch at the apex. Fix batten Q to the inside face of the front panel so that its top edge is flush with the top edge of the panel and with a 25mm gap at either end as shown in Fig.4.

Fix battens M and N to the inside face of the middle gable panel so that their top edges are flush with the top edges of the panel and so that their two ends touch at the apex. Fix batten P to the inside face of the middle gable panel so that its bottom edge is flush with the bottom edge of the panel and with a gap of 25mm at either end.

In the lower roof panel, drill four 4mm diameter holes 12mm in from the rear and side edges of the panel. Apply adhesive to one of the 25mm faces of the batten V and position it

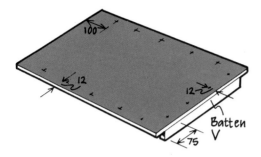

on the upper side of the roof panel, flush with rear edge of the panel and with a gap of 25mm at either end. Screw through the lower roof panel into batten V.

Drill a series of 4mm diameter holes 12mm in from each side of the front and rear panels and the front gable panel as shown below.

Assembly

You will now probably need a little assistance with the assembly. If you intend to keep the Playhouse out of doors for a considerable time, you should glue the panels together with waterproof glue as well as screw them together as described here.

Get your helper to hold one of the sides upright while you position the rear panel, battens on the inside, against the back of batten A, so that it is level top and bottom with

the side panel. There should be no gap between the edge of the rear panel and the inside face of the side panel. Screw through the rear panel into batten A.

Repeat this operation with the other side panel. The unit should now stand up by itself, enabling you to position the front panel, battens on the inside, and screw through the front panel into battens D. You can now slide the lower roof panel into position along battens E with batten V on top and at the back. Do not screw down yet.

Locate the front gable panel, battens on the inside, so that its bottom edge is flush with the bottom of battens C (175mm down from the top of the side panel). Pull the lower roof panel forward until batten V is tight up *behind* the lower gable panel. Then screw through the holes at the bottom of the lower gable panel into batten V and check that the unit is square. Provided that it is, and making sure that the side panels are pulled tightly together so that there is no gap between the lower roof panel and the inside faces of the side panels, screw through the lower roof panel into

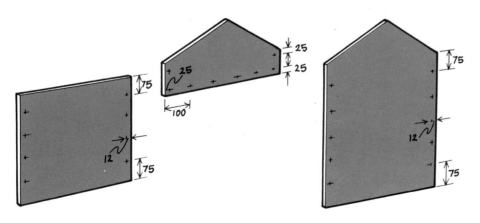

battens E. Drill a series of 4mm diameter holes through the lower roof panel into the edge of batten Q and screw down there as well.

Now measure the diameter of a tin of car polish and draw a line along the edge of the two smaller roof panels, half the diameter of the tin in from the edge. Then mark the centre of this line and draw in the scalloped edge, working out from the central point already marked so

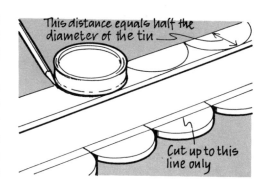

that the incomplete scallops at each end are more or less even. Finally draw another line along each roof panel about an inch nearer the edge than the one you have already drawn and cut out the scallops with your jig saw to that second line.

The overhang of the pitched roof can be positioned over the door or over the front window as you wish. When you have decided where you want it, mark the position of the centres of battens F, G, M and N and drill three evenly spaced 4mm holes through the roof panels and into the battens. Screw the roof panels into place in such a way that a narrow vee-shaped gap is left down the middle. Re-inforce the join by pinning and gluing off-cuts of batten into the apex of the roof from inside the Playhouse. Then close-up the vee-shaped gap by gluing a suitable

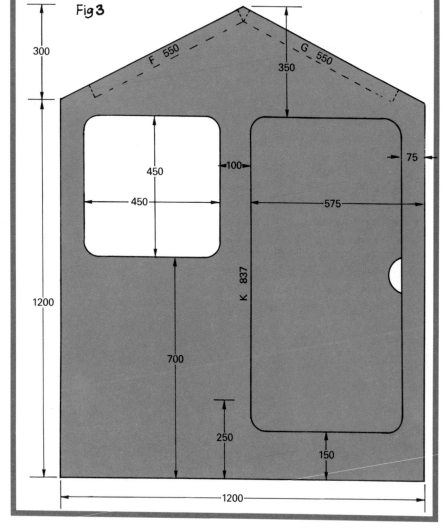

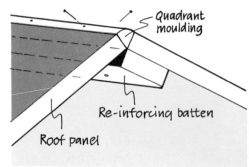

length of quadrant moulding into it with waterproof glue and pinning it to the edges of each panel with panel pins hammered through the quadrant into the roof panel.

The carpentry for the Old Boot Playhouse is now complete. If you want it to be completely waterproof, then all the joints will need to be sealed with mastic as described for the Caravan Playhouse.

Painting

The large size of the Old Boot makes it suitable for a great variety of different paint schemes. The one shown in the illustrations here is only the starting point. You can position the patches and the flowers growing against the walls wherever you like or you could even fix wire mesh to the Playhouse and have genuine flowers growing up it, though they had better be tough varieties.

As with all the outdoor projects, you must not skimp the painting stage or the plywood could start delaminating – the various layers could start to separate. Ideally you should start the process off by painting the outside with a coat of PVA adhesive thinned down with water and while that is drying, you could paint the inside with primer.

When both of those coats are dry, undercoat the inside and then begin undercoating the outside starting at the apex of the roof. You will probably need a step ladder to get to the roof and the top of the sides comfortably so you must work from the top downwards to minimise the mess. With the area of painting

involved here, you will need a good quality 3 inch brush for the job or it will just take too long.

Paint on the finishing coat using the same procedure as for the undercoat. Only paint on the finishing touches, whether they be wolves, piggies, flowers or patches and laces when the top coat has had plenty of time to harden.

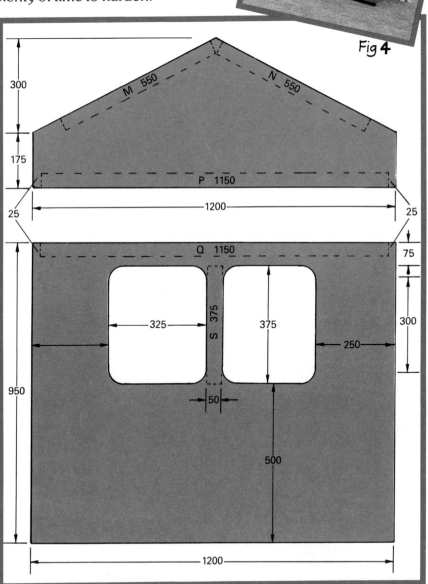

Fig 4

115

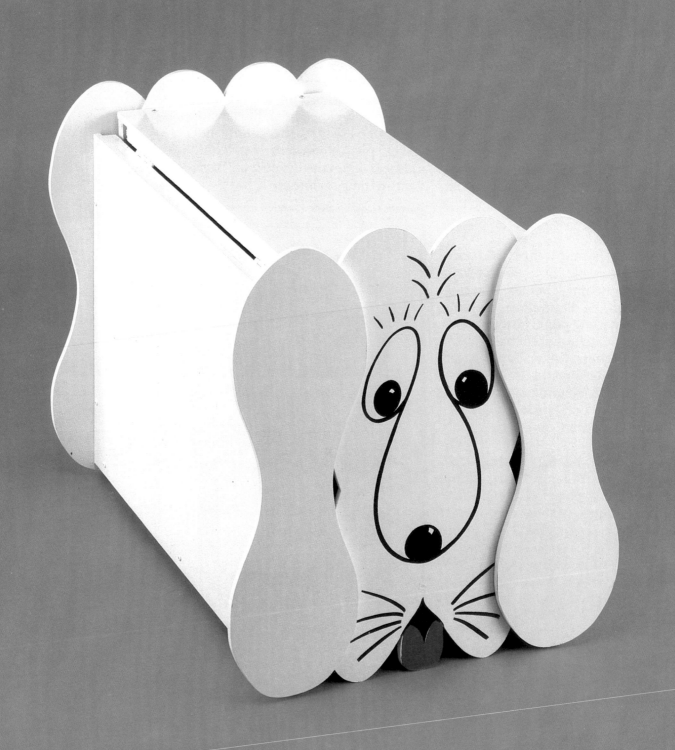

Dog Eared Table

It is unlikely that your children's homework books will ever get as Dog-Eared as this Table.

The Dog Ear table always keeps its nose to the ground to sniff out exciting games to play, and the ears can be extended according to the amount of room needed at any particular moment. But there is a law that says however large the area available, it will always end up piled high with toys and games so there is something to be said for tailoring the size of the table to the room it is going to occupy.

The way to reduce the size of the table if necessary is to cut down the width of the folding sides and the legs that support them. Obviously the legs must remain the same height. This is quite easy to do – the only possible problem is that you will have to draw a freehand pattern to mark out the ears from. Do not alter the size of. the centre section because that could easily upset the stability of the whole unit.

Do not be tempted to build the table out of chipboard because it is just not strong enough for this job and the measurements given cannot be adapted to the extra thickness of the different material without wholesale alterations in the design.

If you want to make the job easier, you could eliminate the folding sides and build the table with a one-piece top instead. The end product would be more rigid but do not leave out the ears if you do this because they are the most important part of the dog's character. What is more they do prevent all manner of things being pushed off the table when it is being used.

Marking Out

All the panels for this table can be cut from one sheet of plywood with some to spare as you can see from the cutting diagram on the next page. To start with, you will need two faces and four ears, so cut two panels 600mm × 300mm and four panels 600mm × 200mm from your sheet of plywood. Draw a vertical centre line on one face of each of these panels. You should do all your marking out (except for the actual features) on the rougher, inside face of the panels.

Draw a rectangular box 600mm × 150mm on your sheet of tracing paper and then draw in vertical and horizontal lines at 50mm intervals so that you have a grid of 50mm squares. The left hand vertical line will be the centre line of the face. So you can now transfer the right-hand half of the face to the tracing paper,

Materials
1 2440mm × 1220mm sheet 9mm plywood.

Battens
Cut from 50mm × 25mm PAR
2	× 350mm	A
4	× 425mm	B,C
2	× 100mm	D
2	× 650mm	F,G
4	× 725mm	H,J
4	× 400mm	K
4	× 525mm	L

11m of battening allowing for some waste.
Cut from 100mm × 25mm PAR
1	× 700mm	E

4 or preferably 6 75mm hinges.
2 50mm × 25mm hinges.
2 38mm × 38mm hinges.
25 no.8 panhead screws.
4 50mm × no.10 countersunk woodscrews.
50 18mm countersunk screws (for hinges and leg assemblies).
1 600mm × 800mm sheet of tracing paper.
4 A4 sheets carbon paper.

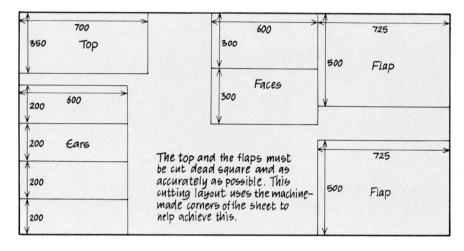

The top and the flaps must be cut dead square and as accurately as possible. This cutting layout uses the machine-made corners of the sheet to help achieve this.

including the features. One square on your tracing paper represents one large square on the drawing. The bottom of the jowls are on the bottom line and the top of its head touches the top line.

When you are happy with the design, lay your carbon paper (carbon side down) to the right of the centre line on the inside face of one of the 600mm × 300mm panels. Lay the tracing paper on top of the carbon paper so that the left-hand line of your box is on the centre line of the panel. Then trace in the outline of the right-hand side of the face. Do not trace in the features at this stage. Now move the carbon paper to the left-hand side of the centre line, turn the tracing paper over, line up the centre line and trace in the left-hand side of the face. Repeat this procedure on the inside face of the other 600mm × 300mm panel.

Next, draw in a 600mm × 100mm rectangular box on your tracing paper and divide it up into 50mm squares as before. The left

hand line is the centre line of the ear(s) and the top line is the top of the ear. You will notice that the ears are shorter than the face. This is important – do not extend the size of the ears or they will scrape on the ground when you open up the table. Transfer the outline of the right-hand side of the ear to your tracing paper, remembering that one of your 50mm squares equals one large square on the drawing. You can now transfer the shape of the ear to the inside faces of the 600mm × 200mm panels, lining up with the centre line and the top of the panel and, turning your tracing paper over, trace in the left-hand side of the ear. Go through this process for all four ears.

You must now mark the position of battens A, B, C, and D on the inside face of these panels BEFORE you cut out the shapes. So, on the inside of the face panels draw a horizontal line 60mm down from the top of the panel. This will indicate the position of the top of batten A. On the centre line of all four ear panels, mark a point Z 125mm down from the top of the panel (which should also be the top of the ear). Then arrange the ear panels in two pairs and mark them L1 and R1 and L2 and R2.

On the inside face of the ear marked R1 draw a line parallel to the centre line and 25mm to the left of it. On the ears marked L (for left) draw a line parallel to the centre line and 25mm to the right of it. These lines will give you the position of the inside edge of battens B and C. If these battens were exactly 50mm

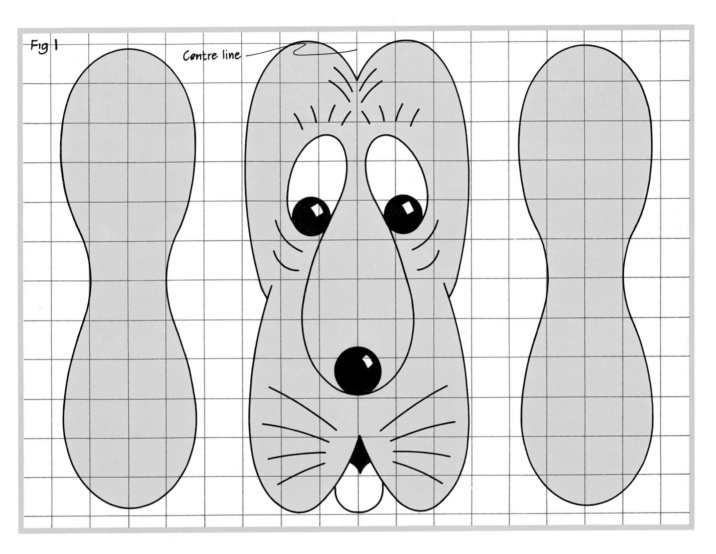

Fig 1

Centre line

wide they would be exactly central on the ears, but since they have been planed to less than 50mm they have to be off-set to one side slightly to compensate for this.

Mark ears R2 and L2 the other way round and then go ahead and cut out all four ears with your jig saw. Smooth off the edges with sandpaper.

Finally, cut out two rectangular panels 500mm × 725mm and one rectangular panel 350mm ×

700mm. It is important that all the corners of these panels are right angles or the table will end up out of square! Cut to the outside of your pencil lines so that the *finished* sizes are 500mm × 725mm and 350mm × 700mm exactly.

Battens
Cut the battens to the lengths shown at the beginning of this section. Sand and bevel the edges and corners according to their position.

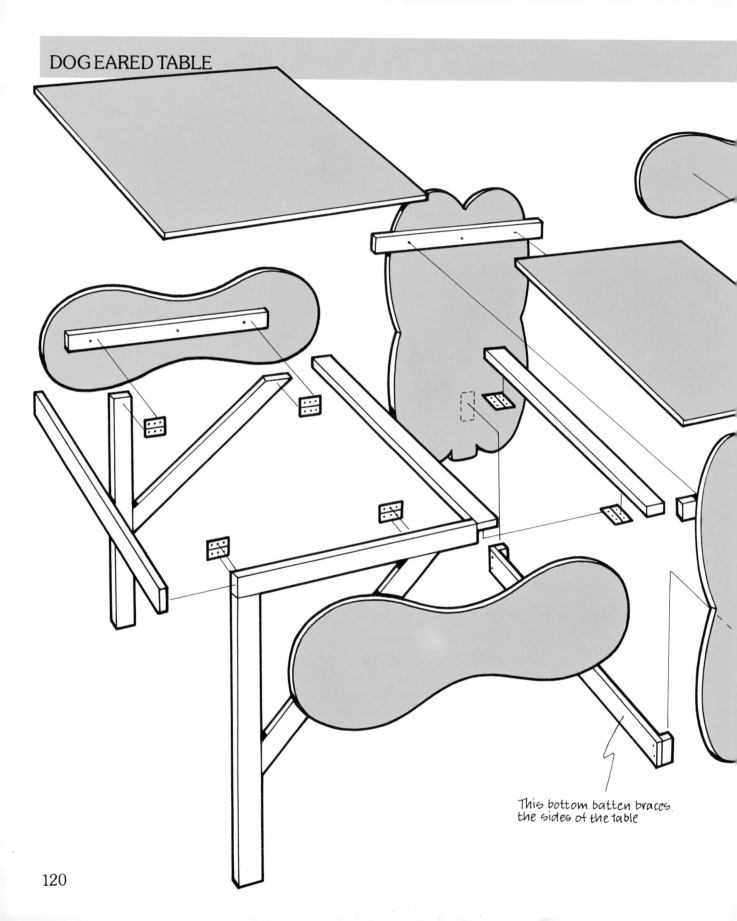

This bottom batten braces
the sides of the table

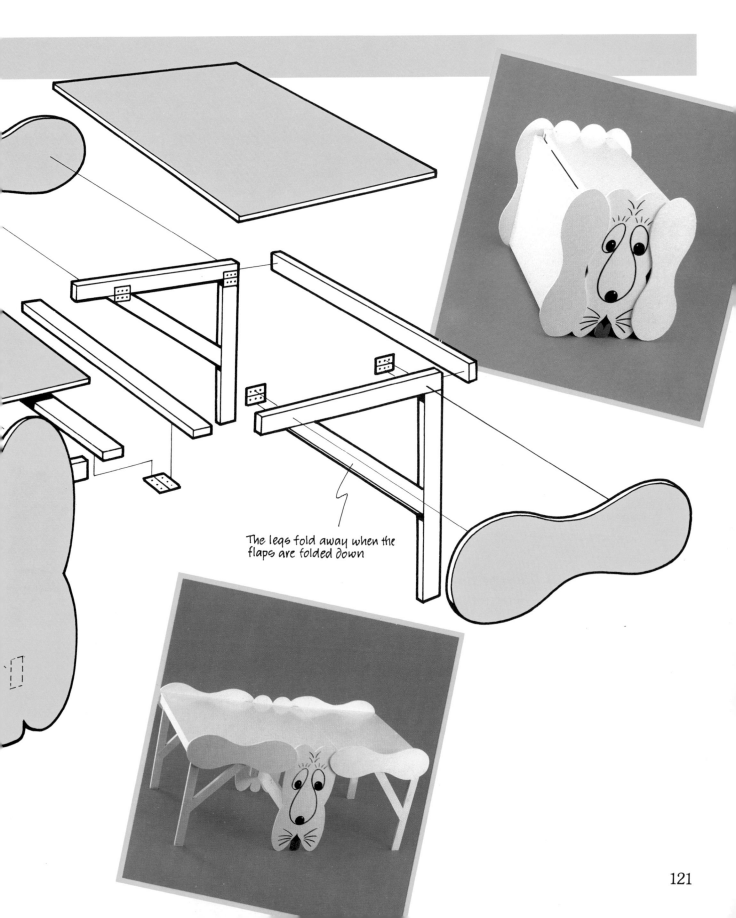

The legs fold away when the flaps are folded down

Drill three 4mm diameter holes through the centre of the 50mm faces of battens A, one hole in the middle and the others 60mm in from either end. Glue and screw battens A in position so that their top edges are on the lines you drew 60mm down from the top of the face, and so that they extend exactly 175mm either side of the centre line. Drill 4mm diameter holes through the 50mm face of battens D 12mm in from either end. Fix battens D in position as shown in Fig.2. bearing in mind that battens D must be fixed on the same side of the centre line when the face panels are back to back.

Drill two 4mm diameter holes 12mm in from either end of batten E. Then screw and glue batten E to battens D, so that the ends of batten E are right up against the inside faces of the face panels. This assembly should now stand up by itself.

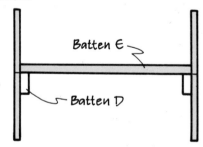

Batten E

Batten D

Drill three 4mm diameter holes through the 50mm face of battens F, G, H, one hole 50mm in from either end and one in the middle. Fix battens F and G to the underside (rougher side) of the top panel, 25mm in from either side and with their outer edges flush with the edge

of the panel. Fix batten H to the underside (rougher side) of the table flaps so that it fits along one of the 725mm sides of the panel.

Now turn these three panels over so that the battens are on top and lay them together so that batten F is in contact with one batten H and batten G is in contact with the other batten H. Mark the centre of battens F, G and H and line up these marks.

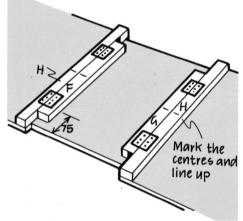

H

F

75

G

H

Mark the centres and line up

Assembly
Lay a pair of 75mm hinges in position evenly-spaced along each side of the table and mark the centre of the holes. Then make a starter hole with a nail or a bradawl. Drill with a 2mm diameter bit to a depth of about 12mm and screw the hinges into place. Hold the battens close together as you do this.

You can now turn this assembly over again and drop it into place so that the sides of the top panel are sitting on top of battens A. Drop the flaps down. Then you can check that the edges of the top panel are flush with the ends of battens A at both ends. They should be if you have cut the battens and the top

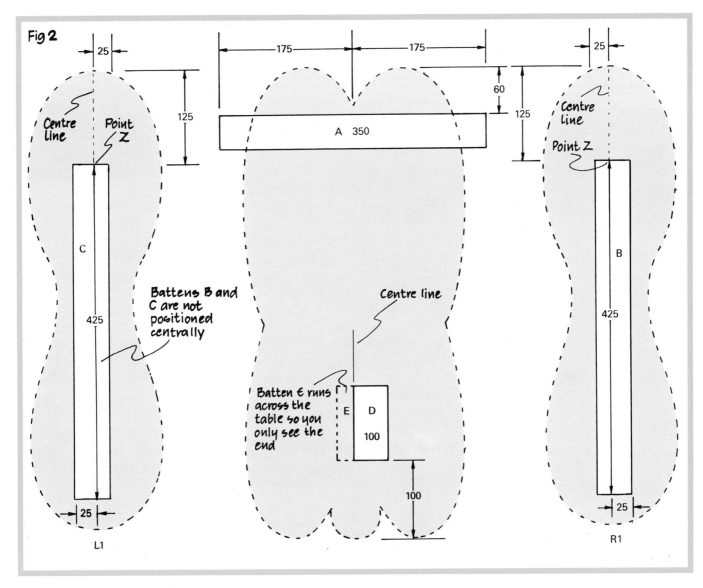

Fig 2

Centre line

Point Z

Battens B and C are not positioned centrally

C

425

25

25

L1

175 175

A 350

60

125

125

Centre line

Batten E runs across the table so you only see the end

E D 100

100

Centre line

Point Z

B

425

25

25

R1

panel accurately. It does not matter if the battens are slightly short, but it will matter if they are too long as this will prevent the table closing.

Now drill two 4mm diameter holes 12mm in from the sides of the top panel and 25mm in from either end into battens A making sure that the sides of the top panel are tight up against the inside faces of the

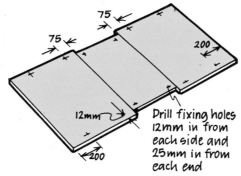

75

75

200

12mm

200

Drill fixing holes 12mm in from each side and 25mm in from each end

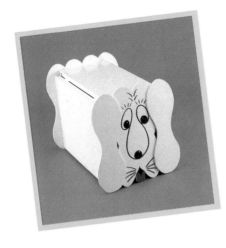

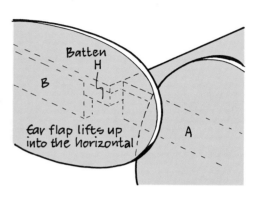

face panels. Screw down through the top panel into battens A.

Drill two holes 12mm in from each side of both flaps, one hole 75mm in from the hinge end and the other 200mm in from the other end. Drill two 4mm diameter holes 50mm in from either end of battens B and C. Fix battens B to the inside of ears R1 and R2 and battens C to the inside of ears L1 and L2 with the top end of the battens at point Z (125mm down from the top of the ear) and with their inside edges on the lines 25mm over from the centreline in the way already described.

Fig.2 shows the position looking at the table from the side and therefore the wrong way round when it comes to fixing the ears on to the flaps. They will be screwed into place later with the battens at the back so L1 and L2 will be at the left of the face as you look at it and R1 and R2 will be at the right. With the battens at the back, therefore, the battens B and C will be slightly offset towards the top or outside edge.

Position the face panel towards you and take ear R1 with batten B at the back and position it so that the back of the ear is against the edge of the right-hand flap. Batten B should be tight up against the underside of the flap and its top end will be tight up against batten H. The ear will hang down in front of the face and should not be touching the ground. Screw through flap into batten B.

Repeat the procedure for the other side using ear R2 and screw through the flap into batten B again. Then repeat these procedures on

the other flap. When you lift the flaps, the ears will lift up into the horizontal position.

Now place the table on a patch of level ground and then measure the distance between the *underside* of battens A and the ground. This will give you the exact length to which you should trim all four battens L for the legs. It should be somewhere between 490mm and 500mm depending on size of battens A.

Prop up one of the flaps using batten L so that its top end is flush with the end and sides of batten B or C. Position one of the 38mm × 38mm hinges on the inside of battens B or C and L so that the legs fold inwards. Mark the centre of the screw holes and drill with a 2mm diameter bit. Screw the hinge into place using 18mm countersunk screws and repeat this all round.

Now mitre the ends of battens K to 45 degrees exactly. Check with your square that the legs form a right angle with battens B or C, then position batten K in place and mark where the ends touch batten B or C and battens L.

Mark the legs A, B, C, D and put a corresponding mark on battens B and C. You must now remove all

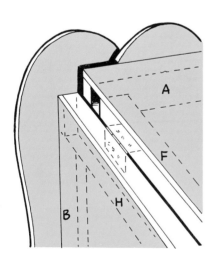

four legs L and lay them out on the bench. Drill at an angle through the bottom of batten K into batten L. Countersink the hole in batten K. Apply adhesive to the joint and screw into position. Repeat this operation for all four legs.

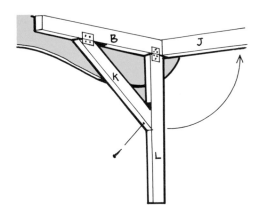

Double check that you have a right angle between the legs and battens B or C and position the 25mm × 50mm hinge on the inside of the assembly at the top of batten K. Mark the centres of the screw holes on batten K and batten B and C. Screw on all four hinges.

Painting

The carpentry for this unit is now complete, although you may prefer to take the top off again and paint it separately. Once the base colour is dry, you can trace in the features using the drawing you already have on tracing paper, and turning the tracing paper over as needed. Be careful drawing in the line that defines the eyes and the nose as the curve there gives the face its puzzled and quizical expression.

As you are aiming to paint this curve in a continuous line, you ought to get some practise in before you get to work on the table itself. Trace out the line on a piece of scrap sheet and try to get the correct wrist action for laying on the paint. Do not use an ordinary paint brush — try to get a signwriting brush for the job that will hold enough paint and is cut off level at the tip so that the painted line varies in thickness according to the pressure on the brush. Use a good quality enamel paint for the job and thin it a little so that it flows without splattering.

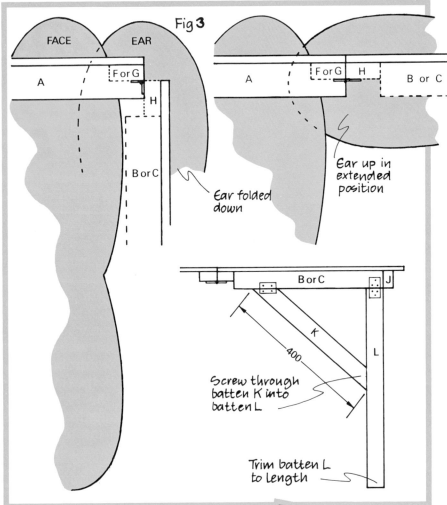

Fig 3

FACE   EAR

A

F or G

H

B or C

Ear folded down

A

F or G   H

B or C

Ear up in extended position

B or C   J

K

400

L

Screw through batten K into batten L

Trim batten L to length

Sentry Box Cupboard

The Guardsman standing at attention on the door will make your children pay attention to replacing things inside.

Materials

2 sheets 2440mm × 1220mm 9mm plywood.

Battens

Cut from 25mm × 50mm PAR

4 × 991mm	A,B,E,F
2 × 575mm	C,D
8 × 550mm	G,H,J,K, L,X,Z
2 × 480mm	M,N

12m of batten allowing for a little waste.
2 75mm hinges.
2 sheets 600mm × 800mm tracing paper.
10 sheets A4 carbon paper.
25 no. 8 screws.

The contents of the toy cupboard are priceless, so it is almost essential to have a Guardsman standing at the door to prevent losses. In the photographs, the Sentry Box is fitted out as an ordinary cupboard but there is no reason why it cannot be adapted to a wardrobe design with a rail to hang clothes from.

The design of the Sentry Box depends on the strength of the door and the quality of the fit between the door and the front panel. It follows that the cupboard must be made out of plywood, not chipboard, and that you must take great care during the marking out and cutting out operations on the front panel itself.

Panels

This project is made up of several small panels cut out of the standard-size sheets. As you cannot hope to cut as straight as a plywood manufacturer, try to use the machine-cut edges of the panels at the front of the Sentry Box and relegate the sawn edges to the back where they will not be so obvious.

You will need one panel 600mm × 1200mm, three panels 600mm× 1000mm, two panels 580mm × 575mm, one panel 600mm × 582mm and finally one panel 600mm × 609mm.

Marking Out

Mark out the rougher, inside face of the 600 × 1200mm panel, in 100mm squares. Each of these squares will represent one large square on the drawing, Fig.1. Then join two sheets of tracing paper together with a strip of clear self-adhesive tape, butting two of the 600mm edges together so that your tracing paper covers the panel.

Lay the tracing paper on the panel and draw in the vertical centre line. Using the squares which you can see through the tracing paper, proceed to sketch in the right-hand side of the guardsman, with the soles of his boots on the bottom edge of the panel. When you are happy with your artwork, cover the right-hand side of the panel with carbon paper (carbon-side down), lay the tracing paper on top so that

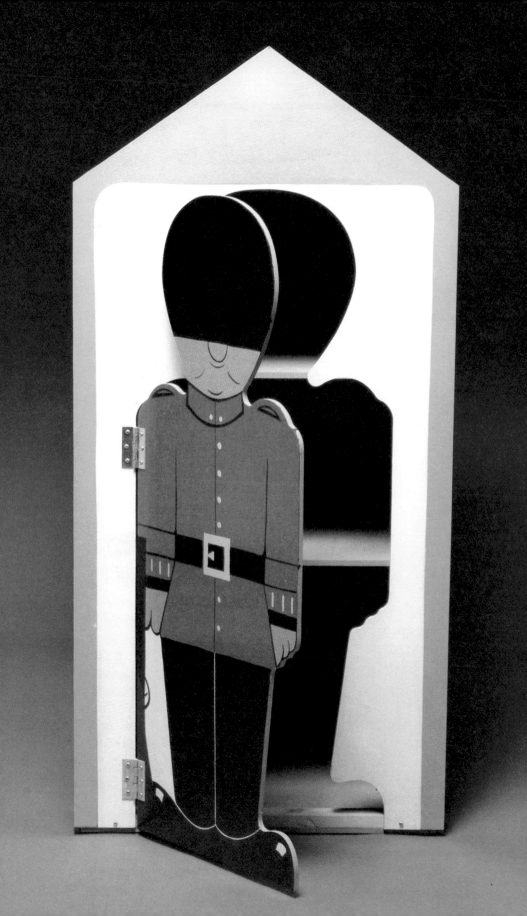

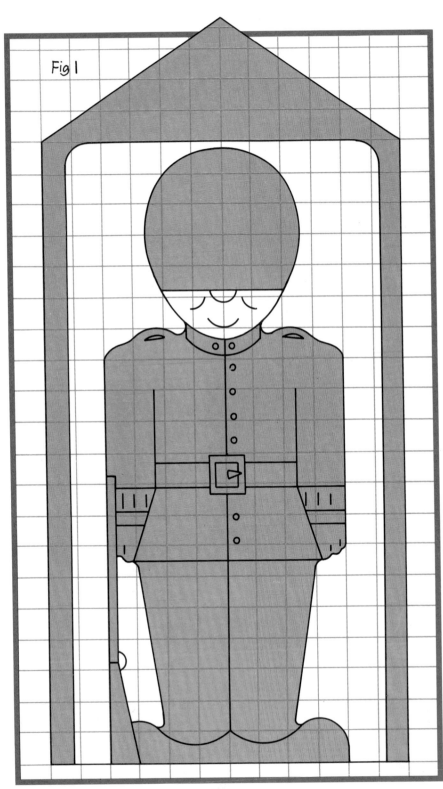

Fig 1

the centre lines are correctly aligned, and trace over the outline.

Now lay the carbon-paper on the other side of the centre line turn the tracing paper over and repeat the operation. All you now have to do is to remove the carbon paper and draw onto the tracing paper (following the squares on the panel) the shape of the rifle.

Next, mark on the panel a line 100mm in from the left-hand edge (the gun side) from the edge of the shoulder to the bottom of the panel. This gives you the complete shape to cut out as shown in Fig.2.

You must cut out round the Guardsman in one continuous line so round off all the corners on the front panel by drawing round a 10p coin to form a radius.

Start sawing at the bottom of the panel around the right boot and keep going until you finish up at the bottom of the panel again beside the butt of the rifle.

Battens

Cut the battens to the lengths shown at the beginning of this section. Sand and bevel the edges and corners according to where they fit into the design. Drill a series of 4mm diameter holes through the 50mm face of each batten, so that one hole is 50mm in from either end and the others spaced at 300mm or so intervals. Make sure every batten has at least three holes in it. Take one batten at a time and apply adhesive to one 50mm side.

Fix battens A and B in position on the inside face of the front panel so that their outside edges are 9mm in

129

from the outside edges of the panel and so that their *bottom* ends are flush with the bottom of the front panel. Fix battens C and D in position to allow for the door as shown in Fig.2. You may need to plane or saw a bit off batten C.

Fix battens E and F to the inside of the rear panel so that their outside edges are 9mm in from the outside edge of the panel and so that their *top* ends are flush with the *top* of the panel, which is the opposite way round to the way the battens are fitted to the front panel. There should be a gap of 9mm between their bottom ends and the bottom of the panel.

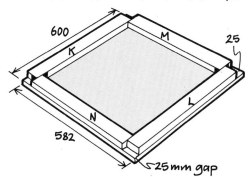

All the battens are flush with the edges

600   M   25
K
L
N
582
25mm gap

is a gap of 25mm at either end. Battens M and N can now be fixed centrally between battens K and L so that their outside edges are flush with the edges of the panel. Build up the top of the cupboard in the same way as the base.

Lay the front panel on the bench, battens on the underside and place the door in position. (Put a couple of bits of batten off-cuts under the door so that it is level with the rest of the panel). Make sure that the bot-

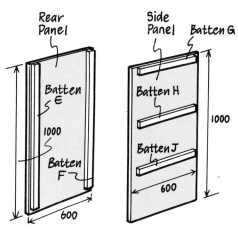

Rear Panel   Side Panel   Batten G

Batten E

1000

Batten F

600

Batten H

Batten J

1000

600

Fix battens G, H, and J in position on the inside faces of the two side panels, so that there is a gap of 25mm at either end. The actual height of these battens is a matter of personal preference, as they only support the shelves.

Fix battens K and L to the longer sides of the base panel so that their outside edges are flush with the edges of the panel and so that there

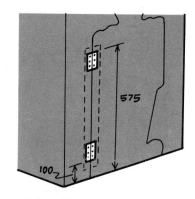

575

100

tom of the Guardsman is level with the bottom of the panel and that there is an even gap all round the door. Position the hinges as shown here and screw the hinges and the door catch into place.

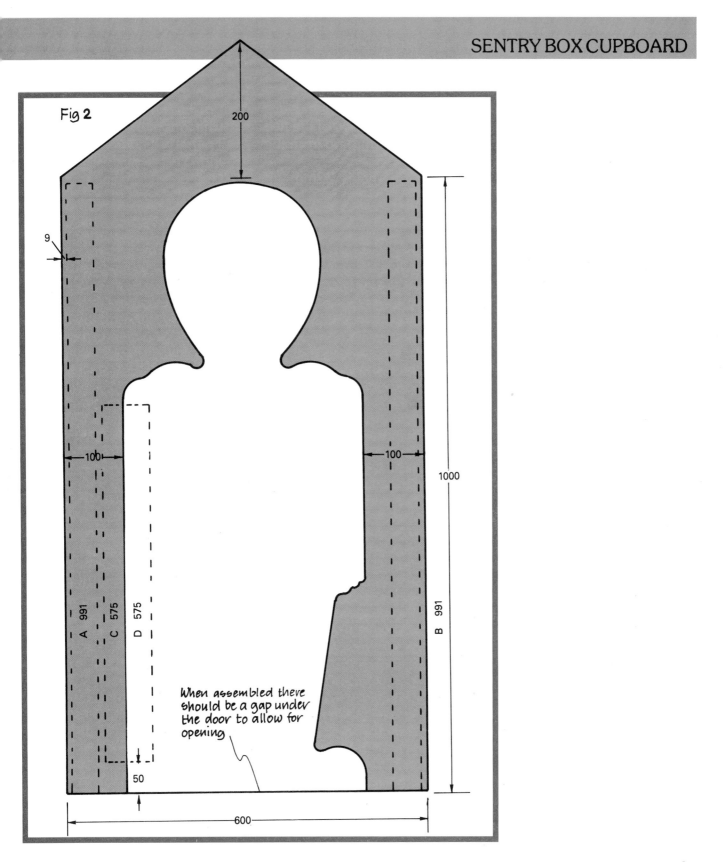

Fig **2**

200

9

100

100

1000

A 991

C 575

D 575

B 991

When assembled there should be a gap under the door to allow for opening

50

600

Assembly

Drill a series of 4mm diameter holes 12mm in from each edge of the two side panels and 22mm up from the bottom edge.

Drill a row of holes 22mm up from the bottom of the rear panel. Position one of the side panels against batten E on the rear panel so that the two panels are flush at top and bottom. Make sure there is no gap between the edge of the side panel and the edge of the rear panel. Screw through the side panel into batten E. Repeat this operation the other side and screw it to batten F.

Stand this assembly on a flat surface and slide the floor panel into position – battens on top. The rear edge of the floor panel will slide

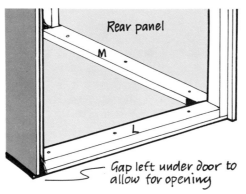

Rear panel

M

L

Gap left under door to allow for opening

under battens E and F until it is in contact with the inside faces of the rear and side panels. The floor panel should be flush with the front edges of the side panels at the front. The underside of the floor panel should be flush with the bottom edge of the rear and side panels.

Screw through the bottom of the rear panel into batten M. Screw through the bottom of the side panels into battens K and L. Now

position the front panel so that the tops of battens A and B are level with the tops of the side panels. The front panel will now be 9mm off the ground. This is deliberate and will stop the door dragging on the carpet when it is opened and closed.

Making sure there is no gap between the edge of the side panels and the inside face of the front panel, screw through the side panels into battens A and B. Drill one 4mm diameter hole 12mm up from the bottom of the front panel into batten N either side of the door.

Position the top panel behind the front panel so that it is flush with the rear panel and the side panels. Drill a hole in each corner and screw down into battens A, B, E and F.

Once you have slotted the shelves into place, the carpentry for this unit is complete.

Painting

Sand all the cut edges of the plywood very carefully, especially around the door where the sawing action may have splintered the wood a little.

Fortunately the whole of the Sentry Box is painted one colour unless you want to add regimental markings to suit a local unit. But the Guardsman himself is quite complicated to paint, though there is no need to use the grim expression on the face of the one in the photographs unless you want him to be a very serious soldier.

You might well find it easier to paint the door if you take it off after fitting and lay it down on a bench on a couple of battens.

Beefeater Cupboard

If the Beefeater cannot keep everything in the cupboard, the portcullis is ready to descend at any minute.

The Beefeater is very similar in design and construction to the Sentry Box and though it may be slightly more difficult to cut out the figure for this project, the cupboard itself is easier to make and so the choice between the designs depends entirely on personal preference, not ease of building. Read through the Sentry Box chapter before you start work on the Beefeater as many of the diagrams and instructions apply equally to both projects.

For a large bedroom, or for two children sharing the same bedroom, one each of these cupboards would look fine flanking each side of the bedroom doorway.

Panels

The Beefeater is based on a series of small panels cut out of two sheets of plywood. You will need one panel 600mm × 1200mm, three panels 600mm × 1050mm, two panels 580mm × 575mm, 1 panel 600mm × 582mm and finally one panel 600mm × 609mm.

Cut out the panels so that the machine-cut edges of the plywood are to the front of the cupboard and the hand-cut edges are concealed as much as possible. There will always be one hand-cut edge on the front panel, so take extra care when you are cutting that panel out. You can also use the machine-made corners to keep the panels looking smart.

Marking Out

Mark out the rougher, inside face of the 600mm × 1200mm panel in 100mm squares. Each of these squares will represent one large square on the drawing, Fig.1. Each small square on Fig.1 is therefore 10mm. Mark out the design on the plywood in the way described in the Sentry Box Cupboard.

You must cut out round the Beefeater in one continuous line so all corners should be radiused off around a 10p coin — by the collar, at the bottom of the trousers, at the bottom of the tunic, and round the fingers. The left-hand side is a straight line right down the shaft of the halberd. Start cutting by the right boot and go all the way round to the base of the halberd.

Materials

2 sheets 2440mm × 1220mm 9mm plywood.

Battens

Cut from 25mm × 50mm PAR

4 ×	1041mm	A,B,E,F
2 ×	925mm	C,D
8 ×	550mm	G,H,J,K,
		L,X,Z
2 ×	480mm	M,N

12m allowing for a certain amount of waste.
2 × 75mm hinges.
2 600mm × 800mm sheets tracing paper.
10 A4 sheets carbon paper.
Screws

Fig 1

Battens

Drill fixing holes through the battens and then fix battens A and B in position on the inside face of the front panel so that their outside edges are 9mm in from the outside edges of the panel and so that their *bottom* ends are flush with the bottom of the panel. Fix battens C and D in position for the door. You may need to plane or saw a bit off batten C.

Fix battens E and F to the inside of the rear panel so that their outside edges are 9mm in from the outside edge of the panel and so that their *top* ends are flush with the *top* of the panel. There should be a gap of 9mm between their bottom ends and the bottom of the panel.

Fix battens G, H, and J in position on the inside faces of the two side panels so that there is a gap of 25mm at either end. The actual height is entirely a matter of choice.

Fix battens K and L to the base panel so that their outside edges are flush with the edges of the panel and so that there is a gap of 25mm at either end. Battens M and N can

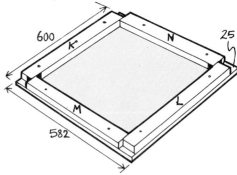

now to be fixed more or less centrally between battens K and L so that their outside edges are flush with the edges of the panel. Build up the top

in the same way.

Lay the front panel on the bench and place the door in position. (Put a couple of bits of batten off-cuts under the door). Make sure that the bottom of the Beefeater is level with the bottom of the panel and that there is an even gap all round the door. Fit the hinges in the usual way.

Assembly

Drill a series of 4mm diameter holes 12mm in from each edge of the two side panels and 22mm up from the bottom edge. Drill a row of holes 22mm up from the bottom of the rear panel. Position one of the side panels against batten E on the rear panel so that the two panels are flush at top and bottom. Make sure there is no gap between the edge of the side panel and the inside face of the rear panel. Screw through the side panel into batten E. Repeat this

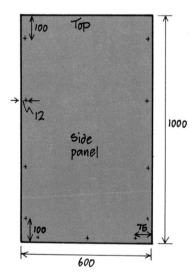

operation for the other side.

Stand this assembly on a flat surface and slide the floor panel into

position – battens on top. The rear edge of the floor panel will slide under battens E and F until it is in contact with the inside faces of the rear and side panels. The floor panel should be flush with the front edges of the side panels at the front and the underside should be flush with the bottom edge of the rear and side panels. Screw through the bottom of the rear panel into batten M. Screw through the bottom of the side panels into battens K and L.

Now position the front panel so that the tops of battens A and B are level with the tops of the side panels. The front panel will now be 9mm off the ground. This is deliberate and will stop the door dragging on the carpet when it is opened and closed. Making sure that there is no gap between the edge of the side panels and the inside face of the front panel, screw through the side panels into battens A and B.

Drill one 4mm diameter hole 12mm up from the bottom of the front panel into batten N at either side of the door. Position the top panel behind the front panel so that it is flush with the rear panel and the side panels. Drill a hole in each corner and screw down into battens A, B, E and F.

Painting

The Beefeater must be painted red with gold insignia and black trimming but the portcullis should be dull iron grey. The stonework can either be limestone coloured or grey-coloured to represent granite. The easiest way to paint the door is to take it off and lay it flat on a table.